CREATING CONNECTIONS FOR BETTER SCHOOLS: HOW LEADERS ENHANCE SCHOOL CULTURE

Douglas J. Fiore

EYE ON EDUCATION
6 DEPOT WAY WEST, SUITE 106
LARCHMONT, NY 10538
(914) 833–0551
(914) 833–0761 fax
www.eyeoneducation.com

Library of Congress Cataloging-in-Publication Data

Fiore, Douglas J., 1966–
    Creating connections for better schools: how leaders enhance school culture / by Douglas J. Fiore
        p. cm.
    Includes bibliographical references.
    ISBN 1-930556-05-5
    1. Educational leadership. 2. School environment. 3. Educational change. I. Title.
    LB2805.F47   2001
    371.2—dc21

                                                        00-055152

10 9 8 7 6 5 4 3 2

Editorial and production services provided by
Richard H. Adin Freelance Editorial Services
52 Oakwood Blvd., Poughkeepsie, NY 12603-4112
(845-471-3566)

Also Available from EYE ON EDUCATION

**The Administrator's Guide to
School-Community Relations**
by George Pawlas

**Coaching and Mentoring First Year
and Student Teachers**
by India Podsen and Vicki Denmark

Dealing With Difficult Teachers
by Todd Whitaker

**Delegation and Empowerment:
Leading With and Through Others**
by Michael Ward with Bettye McPhail-Wilcox

**Human Resources Administration:
A School-Based Perspective**
by Richard E. Smith

**Information Collection:
The Key to Data-Based Decision Making**
by Paula Short, Rick Jay Short, and Kenneth Brinson, Jr.

Instruction and the Learning Environment
by James Keefe and John Jenkins

Interpersonal Sensitivity
by John Hoyle and Harry Crenshaw

Implementation: Making Things Happen
by Anita Pankake

Judgment: Making the Right Calls
by James Sweeney and Diana Bourisaw

**Leadership: A Relevant and
Realistic Role for Principals**
by Gary Crow, L. Joseph Matthews,
and Lloyd McCleary

Making Decisions about Diverse Learners:
A Guide for Educators
by Fern Aefsky

Measurement and Evaluation:
Strategies for School Improvement
by James McNamara, David Erlandson,
and Maryanne McNamara

Money and Schools:
A Handbook for Practitioners
by David Thompson and R. Craig Wood

Motivating &Inspiring Teachers: The Educational
Leader's Guide for Building Staff Morale
by Todd Whitaker, Beth Whitaker, and Dale Lumpa

Motivating Others: Creating the Conditions
by David Thompson

Oral and Nonverbal Expression
by Ivan Muse

Organizational Oversight:
Planning and Scheduling for Effectiveness
by David Erlandson, Peggy Stark, and Sharon Ward

Philosophical and Cultural Values:
Applying Ethics in Schools
by George Crawford and Janice Nicklaus

The Principal's Edge
by Jack McCall

Problem Analysis: Responding to School Complexity
by Charles Achilles, John Reynolds, and Susan Achilles

Resource Allocation: Managing Money and People
by M. Scott Norton and Larry K. Kelly

Staff Development: Practices that Promote
Leadership in Learning Communities
by Sally Zepeda

Student Guidance and Development
by Mary Ann Ward and Dode Worsham

Thinking Through the Principalship
by Dianne Ashby and Sam Krug

Urban School Leadership: Issues and Strategies
by Eugene Sanders

What Schools Should Do to Help Kids Stop Smoking
by William Fibkins

**Working in a Legal and Regulatory Environment:
A Handbook for School Leaders**
by David J. Sperry

Written Expression: The Principal's Survival Guide
by India Podsen, Charles Allen, Glenn Pethel,
and John Waide

ABOUT THE AUTHOR

Douglas J. Fiore, Ph.D., a former teacher and principal of two schools, is currently on the faculty of the State University of West Georgia. He is the author of numerous journal articles and has presented at numerous national conferences. He is the coauthor with Todd Whitaker of *Dealing with Difficult Parents (and with Parents in Difficult Situations)* and is also working on a textbook in the area of School-Community Relations. Doug is married to Lisa, his wife of 12 years. They have three daughters, Meagan, Amy, and Katherine.

TABLE OF CONTENTS

PREFACE

I have been, and I continue to be, a student of our schools. My role has changed over the years, as has a portion of my feelings and opinions about the experiences of schooling. I have gone from being a student to being a teacher, a principal, and an assistant professor in higher education. While these roles may have changed me somewhat, I have had an overwhelming feeling throughout that just will not go away. Schools ought to be places in which students find caring, safety, security, and a compassionate sense of family. This was true long before my educational journey began, and it has become, in many ways, even more true today. For, these things which school ought to be, are sadly becoming alien concepts with more and more students, as each year passes.

When students are able to find the caring, safety, security, and compassion they deserve, then our schools will have created a culture in which learning will flower endlessly. We all know this, yet in our struggles to deal with the powerful issues of "accountability," "reform," and "improvement," we too quickly forget. I write this book, so that I cannot forget. My goal, as you read it, is that you become unable to forget, as well.

This book comes at a time when the shouts and cries for school improvements and reforms are almost deafening. It comes at a time when many people believe that the answers we all seek for educational improvement, in all of its forms, lie in standards and accountability. I offer a different perspective. Without question, our students need and deserve challenging standards. Furthermore, the adults in these students' lives (parents, teachers, school staff, community members, and educational leaders) must be held, in union with the student, accountable for achievement and success. It is unreasonable, however, to expect people to flourish in a culture that is disconnected and mired in negativity.

I hope this book helps you understand the power of a positive school culture. I hope that it assists you, the educational leader, in discovering new and powerful ways to improve the culture of your school. Finally, I hope it affirms for you all of the positive things you already do on behalf of children. We can continue to improve our schools. We will do it more readily when we create, foster, and sustain positive cultures as the foundation of positive school experiences for students.

I owe a debt of gratitude to the many people who have assisted me on this journey. First, I thank Todd Shirley for his assistance in gathering some of the background research for this project. I thank Bob Sickles for believing in the value of this project, and for having faith in my ability. I appreciate the mentoring I received from Dr. Todd Whitaker, a true leader who first introduced me to the power of positive school cultures. I owe thanks to the staffs and families at the three schools I was privileged to work in. In particular, I thank three educators, Liz Douglas, Doug Hollar, and Greg Karas. Much of what I believe, I learned from you.

Finally, thanks and unending love to Lisa. After already enriching my life in so many ways, you took on a new role in this project. You became an editor, and I am grateful for your insight and your overwhelming support of my ideas.

To you, the reader, I am most grateful. You hold the keys to improving our schools. The keys, I believe, are in good hands.

Douglas J. Fiore, Ph.D.
May 12, 2000

INTRODUCTION

THE RELEVANCE OF POSITIVE SCHOOL CULTURES

My experiences in the public schools, both as a teacher and as an administrator, have allowed me to see a certain, albeit it narrow, picture of public education in America. Having these experiences in only three different schools, though they differed in so many ways from each other, necessitated that I could not see or understand all that went into defining schooling.

The experiences I had as a student in higher education institutions helped to expand that view somewhat. Earning both a Bachelor of Arts degree and a Master of Science degree in Elementary Education gave me insights into the lives and significance of teachers that broadened what I previously knew. A post-Master's add-on certificate and subsequent Doctor of Philosophy degree in Administration and Supervision gave me "new eyes" with which to view education. I was experiencing more and studying more. Still, however, there was much that I did not completely understand.

Working in higher education in a completely different region of the country than the one I had grown to know has expanded my view and understanding considerably more. The nature of my position here, much like the work I did in completing my dissertation, has allowed me to visit scores of schools and talk with their students and staff members. I understand much more now, but still feel that the mystery of success and failure in public education remains somewhat elusive. The reason for this, I have concluded, is because of an inability or strong denial on the part of so many educators to examine the one element of their schools that forms the foundation for everything, good and bad, that they experience. This powerful element is school culture, and its power lies in the connections between people that are so much a part of it.

School culture is the system of beliefs, values, norms, and expectations that governs the feelings and subsequent behaviors of all school constituents. It is the culminating result of the collective understandings and ways in which many people see things, but it becomes, in many ways, a singular concept. Traditions, rituals, and expectations are formed and strengthened, as a school culture becomes deeper and more fortified. Over time, many behaviors of constituents become automatic due to the culture that is supporting or enabling them.

Depending on a variety of factors, school cultures can become positive, negative, or something in-between. When they are positive, and research and common practice confirm this, then connections are created and great things are known to happen in schools. Schools with positive cultures experience greater levels of staff contentment and morale, many positive comments from parents and other community members, a sense of collegiality that verifies the old adage of the whole being greater than the sum of all its parts, and an increase in student achievement, both formally measured and informally observed. These schools are powerful institutions that radiate a positive sense of purpose. The only way to understand the power of a positive culture is to experience it. When you do, as I have had the fortune to do on many occasions, then you know you have experienced education as it ought to be. Students learn and enjoy learning, teachers teach and enjoy teaching, principals lead and enjoy leading, and parents support and enjoy supporting. These schools are not "pie in the sky" dreams. They exist. More importantly, transformations are possible to make all school cultures powerful, thereby dramatically increasing the breadth of their existence.

As you read this book, you will read about examples of schools with very positive cultures. You will gain a deeper understanding of why positive cultures and their connections to people are necessary. Furthermore, you will learn specific behaviors, which are associated with the creation, fostering, and sustenance of positive school cultures. All you are asked to do is listen. Listen to your heart as you read these chapters. Pause often to ask yourself if the elements of culture being described are present in your schools. Listen to your mind as you read about the behaviors necessary to bring about positive cultural transformations. Put it all together and begin to create the kinds of schools our students deserve.

If we as educators continue to focus on "reforms of the day" without examining the supporting structure of our school culture, we are doomed for another era of trial and error. We are further doomed to increased criticism, as the public decides that we do not really know how to improve our schools. This is not a knock on all reform efforts. In fact, many of them have worked in many of our schools. When they have worked, however, it was due to the fact that the existing school culture was supportive of such a reform, or at least there was a willingness to transform the culture to make the reform work. When reform efforts fail, it happens because there is a mismatch between the reform's goals and the beliefs and goals of the school community. There is, simply put, no connection. Why do we continue to let that happen?

If school leaders, and I use that term broadly to describe educators from many stakeholder groups, learn to listen to the culture of their schools, then they will have accomplished a necessary first step. If they purposefully strengthen the culture of their schools through their behaviors, then they will have taken the next step. Very quickly, two steps on the journey toward creating powerful school cultures will have been taken. We know that the journey of a thousand miles begins with a single step. With these initial steps, we will all be twice as far along our journey.

Join me as the journey begins. And never forget that our students deserve the best schools we can give them. Too many of them are wallowing in schools with negative cultures. These negative cultures have made too many students feel disconnected. Together, we can reconnect and turn these students back toward learning. Let the journey begin.

1

EXAMINING SCHOOL CULTURE: STRENGTHENING CONNECTIONS

The achievement of American public school students is scrutinized on a daily basis in the mass media and around the typical American family's dinner table. Similarly, the achievement of our students in comparison with that of their counterparts in other major, industrialized nations is fodder for newspapers, popular magazines, scholarly publications, and barbershops and beauty salons all across our nation. These debates and this public scrutiny are causes of great concern to committed educators in schools from coast to coast. The message being sent is clear. Those of us who earn our livings educating children in this nation's public schools must be held accountable for our perceived successes and failures. With so many different factors influencing student achievement, is such a demand reasonable and fair? Regardless of the position any of us take on the issues raised by the previous question, the demand is there, and the fate of American public education lies squarely, though precariously, in our hands.

While this public scrutiny of our effectiveness as an educational system has been heating up and growing, so too has the research on the effects healthy, positive school cultures have on student achievement. Many noteworthy educational researchers have been giving serious examination to school culture as an answer to our supposed demise in education. Practitioners, those whose significant work has a daily, direct impact on students and their lives, have been discovering the power of positive cultures, as well. This is excellent news since school culture, in all of its forms and with all of its variables, is well within our power to influence.

These same researchers and practitioners have concluded that students achieve more in schools with positive cultures. In Chapter 2, this phenomenon is discussed at greater length and in greater detail. Now, think carefully about the two previously mentioned ideas for a moment: We have direct and lasting influence over the creation and sustenance of positive cultures in our schools. These positive cultures, in turn, lead to greater achievement by students. This leaves one very important question. If we cannot control all of the factors relevant to student success, which is obviously a gross understatement, should we not at least control those that we can? School culture is, as this book will illustrate, well within our control. Each of us possesses the power to create, foster, and sustain positive cultures in which our students can and do learn. We have the power. Furthermore, and more importantly, we have the obligation to do so.

GETTING US ALL
ON THE SAME PAGE

Definitions of culture, particularly in an educational context, have increasingly been finding their way into popular literature and conversations regarding organizational improvement. Though most definitions contain similar elements and are consequently somewhat congruent, sorting through them all and arriving at a common understanding can be a challenge. It is an important task, though, because until we all are on the same page regarding what school culture means and all it encompasses we cannot begin to understand our influence over it or our relationship with it. In giving you the following definitions and citations, my intent is to relate them in a way that causes you to consider their messages within the context of your own school. By relating definitions of school culture to our own school experiences, we are better able to fully understand this powerful, important concept. Think of and reflect on your school experiences, and join me on this short journey toward a better understanding of school culture.

School culture is manifest in school structures such as how students or teachers are grouped for learning or work and what their relative social positions are (Cicourel, 1974). School culture consists of the commonly held beliefs of teachers, students, and principals that guide such characteristic behaviors as learning activities, grouping practices, and the way that teachers talk with each other and evaluate student achievement (Heckman, 1993).

These two definitions point to the grouping and social interaction aspects of culture. As such, they are worth noting and are relevant to our work in schools. Think, now, of your own particular school. What are the grouping patterns? In other words, do teachers of similar subject matter tend to flock together, or do they group themselves more on the basis of age and experience? Do you work in an environment where virtually all staff members enjoy collegial relationships, or are there cliques among your staff members? How about your students? Are they in grade levels, which are isolated from one another? Do students spend the day with others of like ability? Are students isolated because they feel that they do not fit in with others? Your answers to these questions tell you something important about the culture of your school, in light of these definitions.

Deal and Kennedy (1982) use culture as a metaphor referring to the values and rituals that provide people with continuity, tradition, identity, meaning, and significance, as well as to the norm systems that provide direction and that structure their lives. This system of meaning often shapes what people think and how they act, thus making it an integral part of what happens behind the school's doors. Think now of some of the traditions and rituals in your school. Do teachers tend to gather in the lounge before class each morning? Is it normal for teachers to stay late after students have left, or is the school desolate 15 minutes after dismissal? Do staff members talk about students during lunch and break times, or are work-related conversations off limits? Are parents welcome in the school? Do parents perceive their roles in the same way as you perceive them? Your answers to these questions get to the heart of what Deal and Kennedy are speaking of in this metaphor. These rituals, traditions, and resulting norm systems absolutely do structure the behaviors and attitudes of members of the school community.

This is so true that, as stated earlier, researchers have begun to pay close attention to the effects healthy and sound school cultures have on student achievement, motivation, teacher productivity, and satisfaction. Their studies, completed in schools with diverse student bodies in different regions of the country, point squarely to the impact school culture has on many variables.

Among the many recent studies done regarding the effects of a positive culture is one in which 150 teachers were polled regarding their perceptions of a good school environment. In this study, Sutherland (1994) concluded that morale was high and social and academic growth were continuous in schools where staff and students cared for, respected, and trusted one another. Similarly, Butler (1995) indicated that valuing collaboration and collegiality was an important feature of a positive school culture, which in turn was linked to productivity. It stands to reason that school cultures in which constituents care for, respect, and trust one another will, in turn, be ones valuing collaboration. We have all heard the phrase, "The whole is greater than the sum of its parts." Similarly, I am sure everybody is familiar with the acronym T.E.A.M. (Together Everyone Achieves More). Similar in their intent, these phrases illustrate the accomplishments that are possible when individuals pull together collectively. Therefore, we ought not to be shocked to learn that students achieve more and exhibit greater productivity when the adults in their school work together. As Sutherland and Butler have discovered, this is one aspect of school culture that must be acknowledged and developed.

Leslie Fyans, Jr. and Martin Maehr (1990) examined the effects of five dimensions of school culture: academic challenges, comparative achievement, recognition for achievement, school community, and perception of school goals. Their research, conducted on a large population of students (16,310) in grades four through ten, found support for the proposition that students are more motivated to learn in schools with strong cultures. These results are consistent with other findings that suggest the implementation of a clear mission statement, shared vision, and school wide goals promote increased student achievement (Stolp, 1996). The importance of a mission statement that all stakeholders embrace and believe in will be discussed in subsequent chapters. Likewise, I will address the many leadership roles stakeholders play in developing such statements. These mission statements, it must be noted, are worthless if they are merely a series of words hung on a wall in the school's entryway. Making them much more than that is the responsibility of all members of the school community. Specific roles and methodology will be discussed.

In further attempting to define school culture, we get interpretations from a great variety of sources. Dictionary definitions of culture often point to the term's pervasiveness and totality. *Merriam-Webster's New Collegiate Dictionary* (2000) calls culture "the set of shared attitudes, values, goals, and practices that characterizes a company or corporation." In simpler terms, Marvin Bower (1997) calls culture, "the way we do things around here."

Regardless of the definition we use, the application of culture to schools helps explain why people believe and subsequently behave as they do. In fact, educational researchers have been using the concept of culture to understand schools as sociocultural settings (Smylie, 1991; Morgan, 1986; Schein, 1985; Trice, 1985; Sarason, 1982). It is in this context that we see the need for monitoring these sociocultural norms and beliefs more closely. The patterns created by sociocultural norms can have tremendous lasting power, and should not be ignored. As Deal and Peterson (1999) say, "Cultural patterns are highly enduring, have a powerful impact on performance, and shape the way people think, act, and feel" (p. 4). Because they are highly enduring, school leaders must understand that they may be difficult to change. Existing cultures, we must remember, took time to evolve. Consequently, they will take time to modify and change. Patience and diligence are the keys.

All stakeholders concerned with lasting school improvement need to understand the power of school culture. The totality of its influence and the role it plays in all relationships and decisions is monumental. We all need to clearly see and comprehend the position that culture has in so many of the issues we face in our schools. More importantly, we need to understand our relationships with one another and be aware that these interpersonal and intrapersonal connections we make at school influence not only culture but also virtually everything that goes on in an educational context. If we clearly grasped the concept and specifically knew what each of us had to do to improve culture, then it could become a focal point of our school improvement efforts. This would lead us to focus more keenly on the real problems without continually attacking small ailments. Perhaps less analysis on specific standardized test questions or attendance patterns in isolation, for example, and greater emphasis on molding positive school cultures may be in order as school personnel and the general public attempt to "fix" what ails our schools.

CULTURE/CLIMATE

It is important to understand the difference between climate and culture to best ascertain their effects on a school. While they are often intertwined and are both related to organizational behavior and productivity, their impact on a school's effectiveness may be dramatically different (Sweeney, 1986). The climate of the school reflects one facet of personality and self-image. There is, in fact, considerable evidence that self-image influences the decisions individuals make about their work, the effort they put into making those decisions, and the length of time they persist in the effort (Bandura, 1986).

Culture, at its deepest levels, represents strongly held beliefs, values, and assumptions of a group. The needs and desires of the group result in norms of day-to-day behavior, and impact the decisions made on a day-to-day basis (Kilmann, 1989). A school's culture can be strong or weak, positive or negative. Its deep roots make it difficult to change. It can, and must, be managed, though. For, as this book will illustrate, a positive school culture may be the key in producing world-class schools with enriching environments for staff and students.

Consider the following iceberg analogy. The image created, analogous to a giant iceberg floating along somewhere in the Northern Atlantic, helps students in my graduate classes understand the subtle differences between school climate and school culture. This, in turn, helps them to better understand the dramatic differences in how we change or mold the two. The mass of ice floating in the frigid waters represents school climate. That is, it is readily observable. We can perceive characteristics and qualities of that iceberg in much the same way that we perceive characteristics and qualities of a school. It does not take long to make observations of the iceberg, just as it does not take long to observe the climate of a school.

Now, we all know from our studies in school and from popular movies such as *Titanic* that there is much more to an iceberg than a large block of ice floating in cold waters. Instead, there is a giant mass of ice below the surface of the water that is not visible, or readily observable by us. In fact, this mass of ice below sea level is larger, often more complex, and provides the supporting structures necessary for the existence of the part of the iceberg we are able to see. School culture is analogous to this image. It is the supporting structure on which the climate rests. To observe it and perceive its qualities and characteristics requires much deeper study. The shape of it undergoes slower and more purposeful change than does its more easily observable climate. Likewise with an iceberg, the mass below the water's surface is stable and difficult to modify. It is its counterpart floating above the water that is victim to environmental factors, such as sun, wind, and rain, which can cause more rapid changes. In time, the whole iceberg, including the cultural representative under the water, can be transformed. It takes time, and it takes purpose, though. Understanding this is vitally important for too many school leaders have "given up" in frustration because they were unaware of the time commitment required to change an existing culture. This is one reason why vision is so important. Leaders with vision and understanding, and who routinely espouse the mission of a school, recognize that changes are being made even when they are not immediately visible. These leaders exhibit patience, they do not give up on their vision, and they understand that eventually they will reap all that they have sown.

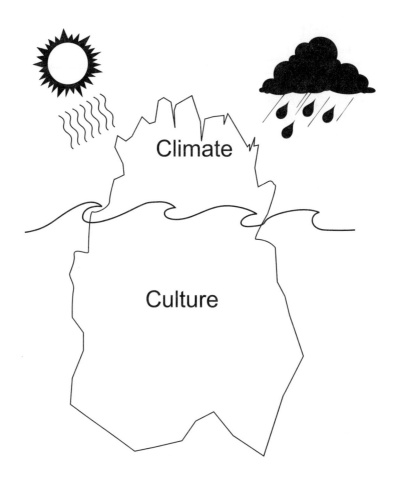

WHY FOCUS ON CULTURE?

With so many educational reform movements focusing energies and studies on structural issues, this is a very poignant, valid question. Jan and John Q. Public, in fact, often feel that schools would improve if they focused more effort on changing tangible things than on modifying conceptual ones, such as culture. Many times, for example, the public advocates stronger curriculum. At other times, their cries are for more rigorous standards for teachers and administrators. Still other times, they focus their dissent on students' lack of preparedness for standardized tests. Despite all this, I have the gall through this book to call for a deeper examination of school culture. This is so because culture is the glue that holds the above-mentioned issues together. It is the common thread between them. It is, in many ways, the tie that binds.

If we begin to think of our schools as giant patchwork quilts, this idea becomes much easier to understand. All of the stakeholder groups, students, parents, teachers, support staff, business leaders, community members, central office staff, and even Department of Education staff are represented by pieces of this quilt. Equally represented are reform issues, such as those public cries mentioned above. As such, it is sometimes necessary to replace some older, more worn out squares with newer, more relevant ones. School culture is, as alluded to, the thread that binds these pieces together. When culture is strong, the quilt is more durable. Ripping a square off of the quilt and attempting to replace it without carefully attaching it with the thread becomes impossible. The thread touches every square and no individual square can be bound to other squares without being woven by the thread. Focus on the culture, and it becomes far easier to focus on these other, more tangible issues.

Michael Fullan (1994) observed that neither the first wave of educational reform (with an emphasis on top-down strategies) nor the more recent second wave (with an emphasis on bottom-up strategies) has worked very well. This is due, I suspect, to the reform efforts' focus on structural changes in isolation. Fullan maintains that reform strategies can only work if we "re-culture" our schools. "Re-culturing" can lead to "restructuring," he continues, much more readily than restructuring can lead to reculturing. Therefore, we can conclude, changes in school structures are less the *means* by which school cultures change, and more the *results* of changes in the school culture. Understanding the culture of a school is critical to successful restructuring efforts. It is the cultural change that supports the teaching-learning process, which leads to enhanced outcomes for students (Hopkins, Ainscow, & West, 1994).

Therefore, through this book, I advocate changing the culture of our schools to create learning institutions espousing ideals of achievement and commitment. In a positive environment valuing collegiality while respecting differences, such cultures will set the foundation for student achievement and growth. This, in turn, will change the entire theory of schooling present in many, though not all, of our low achieving schools. Positive cultures will provide American schools with a new theory of their purpose, which has a shared mission and a renewed focus on student achievement. This is due largely to the relationship between culture and theory. As Thomas Sergiovanni (1996, pp. 2–3) explains:

> Culture is an important factor in improving schools. Less obvious is the connection between culture and theory. The heart and soul of school culture is what people believe, the assumptions they make about how schools work, and what they consider to be true and real. These factors in turn provide a theory of acceptability that lets people know how they should behave. Underneath every school culture is a theory, and every school culture is driven by its theory. Efforts to change school cultures inevitably involve changing theories of schooling and school life.

CONTRASTING CULTURES

In my career, I have been blessed to teach in a school that had a very positive culture. I have also experienced the challenge, during my first principalship, of a school with a more negative culture. Through these experiences, I got a firsthand glimpse of the power school culture has over all aspects of schooling. In looking at a brief comparison of these two schools, I hope to make this point clearer to you. However, I recognize that many of you have had similar or even more profound experiences with school culture than I have. Recalling these experiences will undoubtedly assist you in an even greater understanding of this powerful phenomenon.

During the late-1980s and through the mid-1990s, I was privileged to be teaching at a wonderful elementary school in northwest Indiana. This experience, though I may not have completely recognized it at the time, taught me a great deal about the power of a positive school culture. I saw the impact the principal, teachers, students, parents, and central office administrators had on creating, fostering, and sustaining a positive school culture. Furthermore, I witnessed the benefits students gained from the experience of attending such a wonderful school.

The faculty and staff of this particular elementary school genuinely enjoyed each other's company and worked at creating social experiences to foster their collegial relationships. This is not to say that everybody got along and spent time with each other socially outside of school. In fact, during the eight years I spent teaching there, I had several disagreements with colleagues and saw very few faculty members on a social basis. Nevertheless, at school there was a sense that "we were all in this together." There existed a feeling that, despite our inherent differences in style and personality, we shared a common bond that created feelings of respect and even adoration among and between peers. We understood that we all had chosen our profession because of a common desire to help children grow, learn, and become productive citizens. This understanding transcended any philosophical differences our life experiences sent us to the school with.

This is not to imply that these relationships came without effort. On the contrary, we tried to build collegial relationships. We did this through a few planned social events throughout the year, celebrations of birthdays, weddings, pregnancies, and even the occasional Friday afternoon social hour. On a conscious level, I believe we did these things because we enjoyed each other's company. On a more subconscious level, however, I know many of us participated in these events because of an understanding of the impact our relationships would have on the students and the environment of our school.

The principal, it is worth noting, participated as a colleague in all of these events. Everybody knew that he was the boss, yet socially he was "one of the gang." I did not realize this at the time, but it took skill on his part to create the parameters of these relationships. Nobody ever questioned his authority, yet I cannot say that anybody ever feared him or hesitated to be themselves around him either. Think of the impact that had on students. If my students saw and felt my respect for the principal while also sensing my friendship with him, do you think they perceived him differently than many students perceive administrators? Do you think they looked at him in a more positive light? I do believe that; and I also believe that parents subsequently felt differently about him as well.

This school also enjoyed terrific parent involvement, support, and cooperation. Again, this is not to imply that I encountered no difficult parents during my tenure there. On the contrary, I vividly recall several interactions with parents that were extremely difficult. The overwhelming majority of parents were very positive, though. They contributed a great deal to the school and they supported our efforts, often without question. This was made easier by the fact that their children generally enjoyed school and knew that we cared about them. Let's face it, the easiest way to "win over" parents is to first "win over" their children. Students truly do not care how much you know until they know how much you care. Though there were many days that we had a full house in our after-school detention program, the students of our school knew that we cared.

The superintendent also played a part in the positive culture this school enjoyed. He was a strong leader who believed that the school system we were a part of should achieve great things. He demanded that his principals focused strongly on student achievement, but was careful not to dictate exactly how they did it. This was extremely important, as it allowed our particular school to continue to sustain its own personality. Student achievement, as measured in part by standardized tests, remained important. Whatever honest methods individual schools employed to achieve the goal of maximum student achievement, however, was completely up to them.

Approximately 20 miles away from this great educational experience, I was hired for my first of two school principalships. I saw in this school a culture that was drastically different, but had the promise of improvement. Consequently, I also saw a school that was achieving far less than the school I had taught in. I was excited about the challenge of being an integral part of changing that.

Soon after being hired, I began experiencing some of the tensions that existed in faculty relationships. I learned through attempts at creating a few social interactions that there were great divisions in the faculty. Many of these divisions existed because of events that had transpired decades before. These were old wounds, which had been allowed to fester far too long. As such, they could not be changed simply because I wanted them to. More work was required. This work, I realized, could not be accomplished until I became an accepted member of their culture. I needed to hear some of the stories, take part in some of the traditions, and understand some of the beliefs that guided faculty behavior.

The administration in this school system did little to improve the overall culture. Due to some unscrupulous behavior on the part of some key central office administrators, little trust existed between teachers and administrators. One key person, serving in the capacity of Assistant Superintendent for Elementary Education, did all he could to combat this situation. A powerful, trustworthy, and child-centered individual, he represented the only hope toward building trust between building level staff members and the central office. However, he simply could not do it alone.

For the most part, I was able to ignore the strained relations between the school district's teachers and the central office administration. It did create a minor extra burden in my pathway toward building a positive culture at our school, as such circumstances can hamper many of your efforts. I needed to remember though that I, as leader, was largely responsible for the culture in my school. This point will be further elaborated on in chapter three. Nevertheless, though positive relationships between the district's administrative team and the teaching staff certainly would have been of assistance, a cultural transformation in our school was my responsibility. We need to remember that such transformations take time.

Parent relationships were difficult in this school, as well. Of course, there were some parents who were extremely supportive and involved. However, the majority of the group was as divided as the faculty. Efforts to begin a Parent-Teacher Organization (it had ceased to exist several years before) were challenging, to say the least. Teachers, for the most part, did not want to be involved. Two separate factions of parents vied for power and control of the organization, and attendance at meetings was extremely low. Worse yet, over the years many parents had learned, one way or another, to distrust the school and its staff members.

Students, keenly aware as most students are, of the tensions in the relationships, were more apathetic than I was used to. It was as if they recognized that the adults at school were not, in the least bit, an organized and collegial group of professionals. As a result of this understanding, I suspect that most students failed to see the need for themselves to be friendly and collegial with one another. This apathy led to greater discipline trouble, which, in turn, led to more apathy. It was, as many problems are, a vicious cycle that was difficult to break.

Is it a giant coincidence that these two schools had such different cultures? Was it due to fate? The answer to these two questions is emphatically, No! School culture exists because of the norms, values, beliefs, and behaviors of the individuals who comprise it. These individual norms lead to the development and sustenance of group norms, which become binding and powerful. As such, culture develops over time and can only change over time. It is, as the iceberg analogy indicates, deep and lasting. Consider the overused, but valid educational term, "paradigm shift." A paradigm shift occurs when one's very belief system is transformed. One begins seeing things from an angle never before considered. Changing the culture of a school can be thought of as a paradigm shift for everyone concerned. We all know how difficult it is to get ourselves to change. Changing a group can be that much more challenging.

Still, I believe that the culture of the two schools I have discussed could have, through purposeful development, wound up being very much alike. In fact, I am confident that they are more alike now than they used to be. We must be reminded, though, that changing a culture takes time. Most popular literature claims that it takes from three to five years to make this change. I left this first principalship after only two years. In many ways, that difficult decision I made may have initially negatively affected the culture. People had begun finding themselves operating in new patterns, accepting new ideas. Before these patterns and ideas could become habits, or parts of a new norm system, the school leadership changed.

If the truth be told, I had begun seeing the fruits of my efforts, though. Relationships, in all circles, had improved somewhat. Likewise and not coincidentally, so had student achievement as measured on standardized tests. Still, much more needed to be done. Over time, with consistent effort on the part of leadership and influential staff members, even the most negative cultures can improve. That cultural improvement is so incredibly significant, that it becomes the starting point for all other improvements to build on.

Chapters 3 through 6 of this book discuss in great detail the roles of significant stakeholders in making these cultural changes. There are, this book will show, specific behaviors of principals, teachers, parents, and students that create, foster, and sustain positive cultures. These behaviors will be delineated and discussed to assist you in either transforming the culture of your school or sustaining an already positive one. First, however, let us continue to make a case for school culture by connecting it with student achievement. For it is student achievement that we necessarily focus most of our efforts on. If students do not achieve, in fact, then our school cultures are focused on the wrong objectives and exist for the wrong reasons. This achievement, it must be noted, extends beyond that which is measured by traditional pencil and paper tests. Though obviously important, these measures tell us only what a child knows regarding our stated, measurable objectives. In creating positive cultures, the intent is to show that achievement of larger societal, personal, and interpersonal goals is vitally important to education and the children it exists for, as well.

SUMMARY OF KEY POINTS

- ♦ Many noteworthy educational researchers have been giving serious examination to school culture as an answer to our supposed demise in education.
- ♦ School culture, in all of its forms and with all of its variables, is well within our power to influence.
- ♦ All stakeholders concerned with lasting school improvement need to understand the power of school culture.
- ♦ School culture is the supporting structure on which the school climate rests.
- ♦ Changing a school's culture takes time.

2

IMPROVING THE CULTURE AND ENJOYING STUDENT ACHIEVEMENT

Fundamentally, the only reason our schools exist is to educate our youth. That is essentially why a system of public education was originally begun in America, and it continues to be the sole reason for formal education's existence. Consequently, any book written for educators that does not have the students' achievement, personal growth, and attainment of educational goals and objectives as its focal point is not worthy of the paper it is printed on. I believe that school culture is of paramount importance to the success of students. I further believe that the very essence, or heart and soul, of educational leadership *is* the shaping of this culture. I believe these things because of the undeniable relationship existing between positive school cultures and student achievement. Time and time again, students are achieving more in schools, which are positive, nurturing, and properly focused. In creating and sustaining these positive cultures, educational leaders are engaging in their most significant tasks toward improving, or maximizing, student achievement. The research is clear, and the actions necessary to create environments for student achievement are the basis of effective school leadership.

I assume that everybody reading this book is involved in one way or another with the educational profession because of a love for children and the desire to see them achieve and accordingly be happy. Whether you are an administrator, teacher, parent, student, or other committed constituent, I would hope the above assumption fits. I am also reasonably sure that the typical reader is somewhat troubled by the state of affairs of our educational institutions, at least to some degree. There are surely some areas that you feel are not receiving the attention and/or effort that they deserve and require. A final assumption is that most readers believe, at least partly, that the concept of school culture is intriguing, essential, and deserving of your valuable consideration. It seems logical, after all, that students would achieve more and be happier in schools with positive cultures. My own school experiences convince me that this is so. Is there research to back this assumption up, though? Is there evidence linking school culture to student achievement? What role does each of us play in this equation? Can we master these roles, even if now they appear challenging? The answers to these questions begin below.

ESTABLISHING THE LINK

Researchers have recently compiled some impressive evidence on school culture and its relationship to a school's overall effectiveness. Healthy and sound school cultures correlate strongly with increased student achievement and motivation, and with teacher productivity and satisfaction (Stolp, 1996). Furthermore, as previously stated, the creation and implementation of a clear mission statement, shared vision, and schoolwide goals do, in fact, promote an increase in student achievement. The importance of these ideas cannot be overstated. The implementation of a clear mission statement, shared vision, and schoolwide goals is the responsibility of all members of a school community. We all are vitally important in this regard. In subsequent chapters, I will specifically address the roles of key stakeholders in this endeavor. Make no mistake about it, though. Clearly understood and embraced missions, visions, and goals create the cornerstone for a positive school culture. The challenge is to make them clearly understood and embraced by all constituents. This, in turn, will allow them to become habits. At that point, the collective beliefs, visions, goals, and aspirations make an indelible mark on the culture of a school. Consider the ancient Buddhist wisdom:

> The thought manifests as the word,
> The word manifests as the deed,
> The deed develops into habit,
> And the habit hardens into character.

We must, therefore, make sure that our belief systems and mission statements reflect the deeds that will lead to habits which are positive and productive. When embraced by all and transformed into permanent parts of stakeholders' vocabulary, you will build a schoolwide character that will allow for maximum student achievement.

We all know that students also perform better, when the environment or "feeling" within the school is positive. The overall ambiance of a school is enhanced when stakeholders feel at-home within the school's walls. A climate in which all feel comfortable leads to a productive learning environment that has a positive impact on the achievement of students (Kelly, Brown, Butler, Gittens, Taylor, & Zeller, 1998). This, in turn, strengthens the culture of the school, thus transforming it into a community. Spend time in any school that is perceived by constituents as having a positive culture, and you will undoubtedly hear the phrase "community" used over and over again in describing the environment. This community feeling leads to an increase in student achievement in much the same way that strong neighborhood communities experience increases in the services they offer to each other through a kind of collective achievement.

Consider the concepts of community playgrounds and neighborhood watch organizations that are characteristic of cohesive neighborhoods. As I reflect on the many places I have lived, the greatest sense of community came from a town in which large representatives of all social circles joined forces to build a community playground. With donated supplies and donated labor, we worked in the rain laughing, smiling, and building a playground for the community's children. I am convinced that the result of our efforts, visited frequently by many children, would not have been possible, were it not for the overriding sense of community that guided our actions. Due to an already existing feeling of community, a strong campaign selling the idea to all, and a "kids first" attitude, which permeated events held throughout the year in this community, we all wanted to work together on the playground project. We had, without consciously realizing it at the time, a common mission guiding us. There was a shared vision and a common culture, which underscored our decisions. The whole, as the old adage goes, is greater than the sum of all its parts. When there is an understanding that everybody is "in it together," a community feeling exists and people more readily work toward common goals.

The sense of schools having a "community" feeling is well documented in the research. In Chapter 7, I will give specific examples of schools which have enhanced their roles as "community centers." A related factor emerging from this research has been the indication of an overwhelmingly positive feeling that members of the school community have regarding the school culture. This positive feeling, it is suggested, leads to increased collegiality, which leads, ultimately, to a more effective school. Do you not work better in environments that have a collegial feel? I know I do. This is not to imply that everybody associated with a school must have friendly, collegial relationships with all other constituents. I believe it is clear, however, that a sense of collegiality with some key people makes for a better, more comfortable, and more productive work environment.

In a school community, members are connected to each other for such moral reasons as mutual obligations, shared traditions, and other normative ties (Sergiovanni, 1996). The principal, as instructional leader, is a pivotal player in developing this sense of community due to his/her necessary communications with all stakeholder groups. An instructional leader communicates with people and has a good idea of the uniqueness of the community and what aspirations its members hold for their youth. With this information in hand, the principal can begin to form a clear vision of what an effective school for the community would be (Findley and Findley, 1992). This vision must be consistent with the vision of the school community. If this is not so, the principal, as you will see in Chapter 3, must work purposefully to make it so.

IMPACTING STUDENT
ACHIEVEMENT THROUGH CULTURE

Though collegial, communal feelings make students feel as though they are welcome, safe, and secure, a sense of community will not, by itself, lead to an increase in student achievement. Instead, schools must begin with a core belief system that is centered on the ideal of maximum achievement for all students. Such a belief system, along with a strong perception of community, sets a solid foundation. The following are examples of such beliefs.

- All children can and will learn if given the opportunity.
- Students who work hard should be honored and recognized.
- Student achievement is the core value of this school community.
- Our staff is committed to providing an appropriate learning environment.
- We teach success.
- We are a school of excellence.
- Parents are an integral part of student learning.
- Failure is success if we learn from it.
- Together, everyone achieves more.

Again, a belief system focused on student achievement does not, in and of itself, guarantee that high student achievement will take place. Nor does a belief system, espoused but not embraced and internalized, have any measurable positive impact on student achievement. Such beliefs must exist as foundations, though. Inherent in the human condition is the notion that we cannot genuinely act on something unless we truly believe in it. As such, beliefs like those examples stated above are important prerequisites to a positive culture.

The role of all constituents in creating these belief systems is, therefore, so vitally important. Increased importance and emphasis must be placed on the belief system each time a new staff member joins the school. Many school leaders fail to connect new employees to the mission and vision of the school and are, subsequently, disappointed some years later when the staff complexion has changed and the beliefs, vision, and mission of the school no longer seem appropriate. This is why all new staff members must be introduced to the beliefs, vision, and mission of the school at the onset. Furthermore, and more importantly, the belief system of the organization may need to change, to more closely match the beliefs of the new members. I am not referring to fundamental or monumental changes in the mission. Such a suggestion would be absurd given the large influx of new teachers expected in our schools during the next decade. Nevertheless, it is vitally important for school principals to figure out how new staff members can enhance the already strong mission of their schools. The new staff members must be told that their unique qualities are valuable and will benefit the entire organization. There is not, to the contrary, a rigid set of beliefs and subsequent behaviors that the new members must adopt and adhere to. Leaders who try to force all newly hired employees to "fit into" the already existing belief system are dooming themselves and the school to failure. Our patchwork quilt we spoke of earlier needs new fabric from time to time to retain its strength and integrity. Remember though, that the new fabric must be carefully woven into the quilt, not just dropped there in the hopes that it will attach itself. Moreover, we recognize that the new fabric often enhances, or adds to, the beauty of the whole quilt. The quilt does not fundamentally change when we add a new fabric square. However, it does experience an incremental modification in its beauty and durability.

The modifications of beliefs, vision, and mission lead, in many ways, to complete restructuring efforts in the school. Though they may be gradual, these restructuring efforts must involve the entire school community so that the beliefs, vision, and mission continue to represent all stakeholders. It has become popular to view restructuring as that aspect of school improvement, which involves physical changes, or, at the very least, changes in scheduling and instructional delivery methods. However, changes in the belief system are also restructuring efforts because such changes impact the organization's purpose to a larger degree. In fact, they probably have far more to do with student achievement than do physical restructuring attempts. As Kaplan and Evans (1997, p. 8) note:

> Effective restructuring must have a positive impact on classroom instruction and learning. Changing the high school structure, painting the walls, and putting security cameras in the halls, however, will accomplish little for students' achievement unless the school culture—beliefs about what teachers and students do and how they do it—is also affected. Attending carefully to school environment issues—physical and cultural—can provide a necessary context to essential classroom changes.

There are, of course, many cases on record, of schools that have successfully improved student achievement through structural changes. Think, for example, of the impact that adding science labs can have on the success of a science program. Consider how theater and concert performances can be enhanced when a state of the art auditorium, complete with the latest acoustical features, is added. Imagine the impact on a physical education program when all new equipment is purchased. Lastly, consider the debates raging about the potential, and often realized, impact of changing from traditional to block scheduling.

At issue is not the dispute of whether or not structural changes improve student achievement. Rather, I maintain, the issue involves the impact of such changes if culture is unaffected or ignored. In places where block scheduling has failed to bring about desired improvements, for example, many claim that the failure is due more to a lack of change in the beliefs and consequent methods employed by staff members than by any flaws in the new schedule. If a structural change is made, but school staff members continue to do things the way they always did in the past, then the structural change is doomed for failure.

When people allow their beliefs, values, traditions, rituals, and resulting behaviors to change along with the structure, then powerful transformations can be seen. Consider, for example, an elementary school that adopts a science curriculum that is much more "hands-on" than the one previously used. Will this adoption, alone, create a more "hands-on" science program for students? Of course not. If, however, the teachers reexamine their fundamental beliefs about science and embrace the notion that it is best learned in a "hands-on" environment, then improvement is likely. Teachers will attend training sessions, change the structure of their science lessons to be less textbook driven, and engage in honest efforts to improve. Couple this with an administrative team that removes all obstacles for change and assists teachers in this endeavor because they, too, believe "hands-on" science is better, and the change becomes more powerful and lasting. Now, add committed parents who were part of the planning and subsequent decisions to adopt a more "hands-on" science philosophy, utilize them as classroom helpers or committed resources at home, and the commitment and ease to change becomes more apparent, still. *This* will have a positive impact on student achievement. *This* represents a change in the culture. *This* is what our schools need!

Some would argue that getting all constituent groups, as described in the above example, to agree on the value of structural changes is a "pie in the sky" dream. Such an argument has merit if considered in a context which ignores inherent "cultural" differences. However, if the initial effort is to include all constituent groups in the development of beliefs, vision, and mission, then such an argument becomes weaker. If, for example, I am a school principal who knows that an examination of block scheduling is looming, my first step ought to be to ensure that we all sincerely "buy into" our established mission statement. If we do not, and the mission statement is just a group of words hung on the wall in the lobby, then my efforts must be concentrated on developing a statement of beliefs that staff, students, and parents can believe in. This statement of beliefs must do two things. First, it must support the changes, in this case block scheduling, being advocated. Second, it must represent the collective core beliefs of all constituents. This process may take a while, depending on the school, but it is time spent that pays huge dividends later on. Remember, perseverance and patience are keys to successful school leadership and the continued molding of a positive school culture. It is important to note that school leaders cannot wait until controversial issues arise before examining the schoolwide mission to see if it supports proposed changes. The mission of the school needs to be revisited regularly. The time to begin such revisiting is now.

When a core belief system is established and practiced in a school, then structural changes become much more routine. When the issue, such as block scheduling is presented, all debates must take place with the spirit of the school's beliefs, vision, and mission in mind. Individuals are now forced to argue their positions based on the ability of their stance to advance these schoolwide beliefs. Without such congruence of beliefs, individuals can take a stance based on a position that others don't even understand. It is the mission statement that forces all of our decisions. If our mission centers on such themes as those stated earlier in the chapter, then all questions regarding proposed structural changes get filtered through those themes. Continuing with the block scheduling example, our collective decision regarding block scheduling's ability to advance our mission becomes the basis for our decision. Whether or not I, personally, like the idea of block scheduling becomes an irrelevant concern.

Consider this analogy: If a family collectively resolves to improve their health by making changes in their diets known to be beneficial, then the items placed in the grocery cart during a shopping trip must match this mission. If individual members decide that they like potato chips much better than Tofu, that does not mean that the chips get purchased. Since everybody agreed that dietary improvements were consistent with the family's mission, individual preferences become less relevant.

LEARNING FROM EACH OTHER

Below are two examples of schools that have improved student achievement through a concentration on their school culture. There are, as you will read, other changes that these schools made which contributed to the increases experienced in student achievement. The important consideration is that things were not changed until after a fundamental cultural change had taken place. The foundation, through a focus on creating a positive school culture, was firmly laid before structural improvements were attempted. Descriptions of these two schools are included as examples of the achievement gains possible when culture is a focal point for improvement.

WESTWOOD BASICS PLUS SCHOOL

Westwood Basics Plus School is an elementary school of approximately 450 students located in Irvine, California. The school's mission, written in 1990 and formally revised in 1995, is to "enable all students to become contributing members of society empowered with the skills, knowledge, and values necessary to meet the challenges of a changing world by providing the highest quality educational experience we can envision."

Intending to take nothing away from this mission statement, I suggest that it probably has many elements similar to those found in your own school's mission statement. For example, many mission statements mention enabling all students to become contributing members of society. Others still, refer to providing the highest quality educational experiences possible. What may be different here, I suggest, is that all decisions made at Westwood reflect a commitment to this mission statement. It sincerely does drive all that they do.

In terms of instructional programs, Westwood focuses their efforts on "essential learning, higher order thinking skills, and developing ethics and values." Every student at Westwood has access to the core curriculum, regardless of ability. Additionally, the curriculum is aligned to the goals in the school's mission statement, district standards, state curriculum frameworks and standards, and national expectancies. In this day of accountability, I am sure every reader's school curriculum is aligned with district standards, state frameworks, and national expectancies. Are they all truly aligned to the school's mission statement, though? Are revisions in curriculum made only after careful consideration of the revision's impact on the schoolwide mission?

Westwood Basics Plus School prides itself on its use of group-decision making and appropriate empowerment. The school boasts of extensive parental support, shared leadership, and the involvement of teachers and students in curricular decisions. All of this happens in support of the mission statement's emphasis on "enabling all students to become contributing members of society empowered with the skills, knowledge, and values necessary to meet the challenges of a changing world."

The success of Westwood's efforts is well documented. As the recipient of California's 1998 Distinguished School Award, the school's test data illustrates that students are achieving at very high levels. In 1998, 92 percent of second graders scored in the top two quartiles on the Stanford Achievement Test in Reading, while 91 percent of the sixth graders did likewise. The school's 12-year data on Limited English Proficient student success demonstrates a strong instructional program in which students earn re-designation to "Fluent" in an average of only 23.7 months of instruction.

These accomplishments take place, Westwood stakeholders believe, because of a concentration on sustaining a positive culture, which supports student achievement. This positive culture is the byproduct of efforts on the parts of parents, students, teachers, business leaders, community members, and the principal. All decisions made at Westwood are done in the spirit of their mission. Because the mission is regularly revisited and modified, it truly reflects what all constituents believe. The students at Westwood, according to all available demographic data, are not exceptional in terms of natural abilities. They are exceptional, however, because of a commitment fostered and sustained throughout their school's culture to high achievement.

ORANGEBURG-WILKINSON HIGH SCHOOL

An equally impressive school in terms of its commitments to school culture and student achievement, is Orangeburg-Wilkinson High School in Orangeburg, South Carolina. Several years ago, this school of 1800 students was in need of academic improvement, according to Superintendent, Walter Tobin. The desire was to create changes that would not represent a "quick fix" but would, instead, lead to long-term improvements. The three prerequisites to lasting improvement, Tobin felt, are:

1. Find a principal with energy, dedication, and concern for students;

2. Convince the community that the school needed to improve; and

3. Build faculty commitment and support teachers in holding students to high standards.

All three of these ideas are consistent with concepts that we already know lead to a positive school culture. For example, research has shown us that principals of schools with positive cultures are energetic, dedicated individuals who always put the needs of students first. In Chapter 3, I discuss in greater detail how they do this. We also know that schools with positive cultures are responsive to community needs, have a strong sense of community, as I have already mentioned, and reach out to and communicate with the community on a regular basis. There is also, we are aware, strong faculty commitment in schools with positive cultures. As is the case with Westwood Basics Plus School, this commitment manifests itself in a meaningful mission statement that all stakeholders can embrace. Superintendent Tobin recognized that the first step toward academic improvement at Orangeburg-Wilkinson was the creation of a positive school culture.

First on the superintendent's list was the hiring of a school principal and teachers who believed in the importance of student achievement and who were committed to improving it at Orangeburg-Wilkinson High School. It was a top priority of Superintendent Tobin's to staff the school with professional staff members with a common vision and the desire to do all they could to help children reach their maximum potential. In doing so, he brought a cadre of educators to Orangeburg-Wilkinson who immediately began working together on making fundamental changes. Among their core beliefs were the following:

- ♦ To set high expectations for all students;
- ♦ To not allow students to use poverty, a single-parent home, or any other circumstance as an excuse for not doing school work;
- ♦ To expect all students to behave properly at school; and
- ♦ To focus all of their actions on student learning.

While many schools have beliefs such as these, at Orangeburg-Wilkinson there was an understanding that staff members would settle for nothing less. This made it impossible for teachers or the principal to ever give up on a student. While it was difficult for some students to understand and accept these philosophies, they eventually had to since they quickly realized that the faculty would not settle for mediocrity.

Beliefs such as those mentioned above also changed the culture of the school in other ways. The principal, as instructional leader, could not do her job from within the confines of her office. Instead, she needed to make frequent visits to the classroom. Because the mission of the school was so focused on student achievement and learning, teachers did not feel threatened by the frequency of these visits. The purpose, they knew, was for the principal to have a forum for giving teachers regular feedback on their instruction in support of the school's mission and vision.

The changes in culture at Orangeburg-Wilkinson High School are producing strong results. The percentage of students who met or exceeded the district's standardized assessment reading goal increased from 28 percent in 1996 to 54 percent in 1998. The percentage that met or exceeded the mathematics goal rose from 22 percent in 1996 to 49 percent in 1998. Finally, the percentage of students who met or exceeded the district's science goal increased from 17 percent in 1996 to 43 percent in 1998.

LET'S GET STARTED

The achievements in the two schools mentioned above did not come about because of a change in instructional methodology alone. Nor did they happen solely because of an effort to align instructional objectives with the stated curriculum and/ or the standardized testing program. While such changes are often warranted, they do not lead to lasting, substantial changes like those experienced at Westwood Basics Plus and Orangeburg-Wilkinson. Changes like these happen because of modifications in the culture, or in the very beliefs which guide the behavior of all associated with the school.

The increased focus we are faced with nationally to improve student achievement is certainly worthwhile. There are schools all over the country that have implemented reform plans which have led to some significant improvements. However, to make lasting change in all of our schools, we must focus our energies on an examination of the culture. We must, through beliefs and resulting behaviors, foster the development of school cultures that make student achievement a focal point. The obvious prerequisite of such a culture is the belief that all students can and deserve to achieve. We must create and then sustain these positive school cultures through deliberate behaviors, rituals, and ultimately, through traditions that are based on our beliefs and our mission statements. When we do this, we will not have created something that is prone to fads or "reforms of the day." Instead, we will have created lasting positive school cultures that set the foundation for student achievement.

So where do you start? First, an examination of the beliefs of those intimately associated with your school is warranted. The discoveries from this examination may have little to do with your existing mission statement, particularly if the mission statement exists on paper, but not in the hearts of those who supposedly abide by it. By observing people in your school and seeing how they interact with students, parents, and colleagues, you can get a sense of what they really believe in. Do these observed beliefs fit in with yours? Will they, in your judgement, lead to the achievements necessary for your students? Is there a way to modify people's beliefs so that a unified belief system can be created that allows for student development and achievement? Remember that our behaviors are often a result of what we consider to be true. For that reason alone, we must start with beliefs.

One of the most significant tasks of school leaders' is their role in creating a belief system, or more formally a mission statement, which reflects what stakeholders believe in and which will create situations for students to meet with success. Once this is done, though, the leader's job involves little more than helping stakeholders "stay the course." Keeping people on track is much easier when the track they ought to be on is clearly defined and mutually supported. I know this takes time and leads to frustrations. The frustrations involved, though, are not as great as the sum of all frustrations experienced over time in a culture lacking the congruence of purpose that you know is necessary.

Many educators grow tired of hearing the benefits of a shared mission statement touted as a solution to some of their schools' ailments. I remain convinced that this is due to the fact that so many schools' mission statements have been created in response to an accreditation edict or a school board directive. As such, these statements are often irrelevant, at best. However, when members of a school community, acting as a family, create a mission statement whose purpose is to truly guide their thinking and subsequent behaviors, the lasting effects of these efforts can be monumental. In a school family, these statements must be revisited frequently, particularly in times of stress, to ensure that decisions made abide by these important words. To understand their lasting effect, consider the words of Stephen Covey in describing the power of his family's mission statements: "Through the years these mission statements have created the common sense of destination and manner of travel that has represented the social will, the culture, in the family. And either directly or indirectly, consciously or unconsciously, almost everything else in our family has grown out of it." (1997, p. 74)

Everything; the beliefs, the values, the decisions, the behaviors, and the culture itself grows out of a mission statement whenever such a statement represents a common creation that all members can embrace.

We can and must create positive school cultures for our students. When we do, we make it so much easier for them to achieve and to be successful. We are all in the business of assisting students, not of putting up roadblocks. A negative school culture creates a myriad of roadblocks that we have the power to take down. Though it all starts with beliefs, there are additional tasks that we all must perform to ensure that our schools will have positive cultures. These tasks and the beliefs behind them are explained in greater depth in the next four chapters. By adopting many of them, the task of creating the positive cultures our schools need becomes manageable and understandable.

SUMMARY OF KEY POINTS

♦ Researchers have recently compiled some impressive evidence on school culture and its relationship to a school's overall effectiveness.

♦ Clearly understood and embraced missions, visions, and goals create the cornerstone for a positive school culture.

♦ When there is an understanding that everybody is "in it together," a community feeling exists and people more readily work toward common goals.

♦ We must, through beliefs and resulting behaviors, foster the development of school cultures that make student achievement a focal point.

♦ One of the most significant tasks of school leaders' is their role in creating a belief system, or more formally a mission statement, which reflects what stakeholders believe in and which will create situations for students to meet with success.

3

CREATING, FOSTERING, AND SUSTAINING A POSITIVE CULTURE: THE PRINCIPAL'S ROLE IN DEVELOPING CONNECTIONS

It has been established thus far, that students achieve and staff members are more content and bound by common beliefs in a school with a more positive culture. This, I must point out, is great news for school leaders everywhere. After all, who among us does not want student achievement to be at or at least nearer to its maximum potential? Likewise, are there any school leaders who do not want staff members to feel good about themselves and their work, assuming that these staff members are doing what's in the best interest of students? School administrators in all capacities want their schools to be positive learning environments in which student achievement is at the heart of the institution's existence. We want students to achieve all that they are able to, and we want staff members to come to work each week in a "Thank God, it's Monday!" frame of mind. The questions are: "What is the principal's role in making this more likely to happen?" "Are there specific leadership behaviors that will lead to an improved school culture and, if so, what are they?" And, finally, "Can all leaders be trained to exhibit attitudes that will positively impact the culture of their schools?"

To assist in responding, I ask you to examine the behaviors of three individuals. All three of these individuals are practicing principals, though the schools they lead differ from one another in almost every demographic classification I know of. The daily work these three principals engage in and the responsibilities inherent in their positions differ somewhat, but their overriding sense of mission and the understanding of their roles as leaders makes them kindred spirits.

The information contained in the summaries below represents observations made and understandings arrived at during time I spent in their schools. In studying and examining the culture of these schools, I interviewed each of these principals and several of their staff members. I asked the participants in all three schools the very same questions. In addition, I spent considerable time walking the hallways, and informally observing interactions and relationships among and between school stakeholders. This was all done after collecting survey data, which confirmed that these schools had positive cultures, as perceived by members of their staffs. These interviews and observations were specifically designed to discover why the cultures were so positive and, more importantly, what role the principal played in the success. Though the schools are quite different from each other in many ways, the behaviors of the principals are stunningly similar. As is illustrated below, the methods they employ, the attitudes they espouse, and the behaviors they engage in are remarkably alike. They know how to create, foster, and sustain positive school cultures, and they appear to do it on a daily basis. They share a common understanding that the key to a positive culture rests firmly in the hands of the principal.

THREE PRINCIPALS

PRINCIPAL 1

The first school I visited is located in a town of approximately 8,000 people in a suburban community, which can best be described as "typically American." At the time of my visit, the principal had been in his position as leader of the school for six years.

The principal described the school as a friendly and pleasant place for children. He said, "It is important that the kids be treated with respect and friendliness to start the day off right." He felt that the school had an obligation to treat children this way, particularly because many of them, he feared, did not get such treatment outside of school. He explained that this may be a sad commentary on family and society. He went on to say that, the school had an obligation therefore, to create a sense of family for the students. When asked what he did to influence the school's culture, the principal first mentioned the efforts he makes to model trust. He explained that this is the cornerstone of a positive culture. He felt that individually speaking to teachers when there is a concern, instead of addressing them in a whole group setting, is one way in which this trust is built. Teachers learn to trust that the principal is not out to embarrass, or make examples of them. Instead, they come to know that he is interested in discussing concerns with them in a nonthreatening, private manner.

In describing his typical school day, the principal mentioned that he spends his day "with kids" as much as possible. He said, "Being visible is vitally important to my success here. It helps create that friendly tone kids, teachers, and parents need." It was extremely important to this principal for kids to know him and feel comfortable in his presence.

The teachers I spoke with felt that the principal was responsible for the culture they described as "positive, comfortable, and homey." They mentioned their appreciation of the encouraging little notes that the principal often placed in their mailboxes. These notes were one example of the many ways in which the principal regularly communicated. The teachers spoke of how hard the principal worked and how positive his demeanor usually was. One teacher said, "If it were not for him, this would be an eight to three job for me. Because of him, I work much harder than that because I don't want to disappoint him." They considered him to be a "tireless worker" who was very concerned with curricular improvement.

Both the principal and the teachers referred to the shared governance common in this school building. They all felt that this improved the culture of their school because stakeholders felt committed to the outcomes of decisions they had participated in. As an example, the principal said, "I don't make the agendas for all of our meetings." This responsibility, he elaborated, was left to all those who had a stake in the outcome of meeting agenda items. The teachers seemed pleased with this and commented on how important they felt to be able to lead the staff on certain meeting agenda items.

The school itself had a very inviting environment. Student work was displayed prominently, and there was a real sense of school pride exhibited as I walked through the halls. At the start of the day, a one-minute interlude of soft music played over the intercom prior to morning announcements. The principal felt that this gave students and teachers a quiet moment in which to get focused and ready for the day.

PRINCIPAL 2

The second school I visited was located in a suburb of a large metropolitan area. The suburb serviced by this school had a population of approximately 16,000 people. Forty-five percent of the land area serviced by the school was reserved for a large federal prison, which had been housed there for decades. The neighborhood was described as a mix of "working poor" and "middle class" families. The principal had been principal of the school for the past 7 years, but had been a teacher at the school for 18 years prior to becoming principal.

Stating that her overall philosophy was, "You don't mess with what people do well," the principal described the school's culture as "fluid, active, alive, hands-on, happy, and exciting." She described many curricular initiatives she took pride in, but was quick to point out that teachers initiated many of them. She apparently felt that it was crucial for people to receive credit for the many things that they do well. She said that whenever it was possible she got in the classroom and taught, so as not to forget the feeling. This allowed her to have "empathy for teachers," which, in turn, helped her in proper, thoughtful decision-making.

The principal felt that her honesty greatly influenced the culture. She said, "One lie undoes thousands of honest responses." Therefore, she said that she modeled honesty and acceptance so that other stakeholders would, in turn, be honest with her. Honesty, as we know, is a trademark of positive school cultures.

Being in the building before teachers got there and after they left was one way that the principal felt she communicated, or demonstrated, the importance of hard work. She said, "I require a great deal of work from my staff. They need to know that I'm willing to work as hard as they are." The principal felt that the best way for her to influence the culture was to follow John F. Kennedy's plan. That is, she explained, to hire people smarter than you are, and listen to them.

The teachers that I spoke with felt that their school was "one of the best in the country." This was not reflected in standardized test scores, which they felt were often "overemphasized." The teachers valued the fact that the principal treated them as colleagues. They echoed the principal's comments in saying, "You're never asked to do something that she isn't willing to do herself." They spoke fondly of the open lines of communication and of the principal's accessibility and routine visibility. This, they further explained, made it easy for them to approach and discuss matters of importance with the principal.

The principal's school day was described as "very active." Drawing on the concept of servant leadership, one teacher said, "She spends her day serving us." She was described as always being "visible and accessible." Recall here that the very essence of servant leadership requires leaders to have, at the core of their belief system, a desire to serve.

The school building itself was a very vibrant place. There were many exciting projects going on in classrooms and I got a sense of happiness and contentment while moving throughout the hallways. All students the principal encountered during my visit were called by name, and they all seemed to appreciate that. There were many parent volunteers in the building, and they seemed a normal part of the everyday culture. The principal commented on this involvement saying that it took a long time to create, but was worth it. She said, "The children get a charge out of knowing that this school belongs to their parents also."

PRINCIPAL 3

The third school I visited was located in a suburban community of approximately 35,000 people. Describing the school as having "the lowest socioeconomic base in the community" with a transience rate of approximately 20 percent, the principal mentioned that the percentage of students receiving free or reduced lunch hovered at approximately 30 percent. The principal was in his eighth year as principal of the school.

The principal described the culture as "happy and open." Saying, "We are a school of children," he spoke proudly of the ethnic diversity of the student population. Since many of the neighboring communities lacked this diversity, the principal felt that his students were fortunate to be in an environment that included and valued a diverse population.

The principal mentioned the importance of his office staff in the day to day operation of the school. He said, "I taught them how I think about things," in describing their ability to handle most routine tasks. He summed this point up by saying, "I'm the leader, but they help run the building." This allowed the principal to spend more of his day outside of the office, which he felt was important to students, staff, and parents. When asked how he spent a typical school day, the principal said, "Most of my day is spent in the classrooms, in the hallways, and in the cafeteria." It was obviously important to this principal that he be visible as much as possible.

Positive relationships with staff were mentioned by this principal as key components of his success. He mentioned that he takes time each day before school to personally visit with many teachers, discussing nothing but their families and personal interests. Commenting on the fact that he enjoys positive relationships with 95 percent of the staff, he said, "I focus my energies on the teachers who are going to make a difference."

The teachers I spoke with mentioned that the open atmosphere of the school was refreshing. Two of the teachers I interviewed had worked at other school buildings and commented that the environments were ones in which you entered the school and went right to your classroom to work. This school was different, they claimed, in that there was great interaction among peers.

They concurred in saying that the principal was largely responsible for this culture. They mentioned the principal's capacity for remembering important things happening in their personal lives. One teacher said, "You can mention something to him once, and a week later he'll ask you how things are going. More importantly, you can tell it's genuine."

The teachers referred to the principal as "highly visible." He visited classrooms several times per week in a non-judgmental way. Rather than feeling threatened, the teachers felt "very comfortable" with these visits. They commented that they often pulled him into their lessons, to the delight of the students.

The hallways of this school had a very inviting feel to them. Student work was displayed throughout. The principal mentioned that one of the first things he did, as principal was to put bulletin boards up in the hallways. Reminding teachers about how special they probably felt when somebody displayed work they did as children, he informed them of his expectation that student work would be prominently displayed. He explained that this was now "part of the culture."

Also important to the culture of this school were the many extracurricular events involving families. The principal and the teachers mentioned that parent involvement was a key to their success. The principal provided written communication to parents on a weekly basis, and he felt that the parents appreciated this. He also expressed pride in the positive relationship between the teachers and the PTO.

PUTTING IT ALL TOGETHER

These three school principals share several important commonalties, which enable them to impact the culture of their schools as profoundly as they do. The best news for readers is that all of the things they do in this regard can readily be copied or applied to any school setting. Consider, for example, the principal who put positive, uplifting messages in his teachers' mailboxes from time to time. While that behavior alone will probably not have tremendous cultural influence, it certainly did positively impact the feelings that this principal's teachers had about school. They felt respected and appreciated by the principal, and they, in turn, respected and appreciated him.

Mutual respect, in fact, was a common theme in all three of these schools. Recalling Sutherland's research, as described in Chapter 1, morale is high in schools where staff members trust and respect one another. We also know that high morale often leads to higher achievement. Therefore, it is sensible to assume that principals concerned with increased achievement would want high staff morale. It has, furthermore, been illustrated that there are specific ways, such as the positive, uplifting messages mentioned, for principals to work on this. Is this behavior really that hard to emulate?

All principals reading this chapter do their daily work and perform their required duties in cultures that differ, albeit slightly in some cases, from one another. In fact, the two schools in which I served as principal had cultures which were drastically different from each other in many significant ways. As such, it only seems logical to assume that the behaviors of leaders in these environments would differ. The differences need not be as substantial as some would imagine, though. Consider an analogy of teaching long division to students. Those of us who have done this sometimes daunting task numerous times know that our lessons were not carbon copies of each other every time we introduced this concept. After all, the students we taught were different and had different abilities from year to year. Nevertheless, we would also admit, I am reasonably sure, that the methods we employed to deliver instruction did not drastically differ from previous attempts either. In short, while there are many ways to reach students of various abilities and experiences, the fundamental methods employed in the majority of situations are more similar than they are different. Now, for those of you with a mathematics phobia, feel free to substitute a concept or lesson from the discipline that you are more comfortable with in the above analogy. Regardless, in most cases it should be clear that while there is "more than one way to skin a cat" the methods are not and need not be as different as we sometimes believe.

With the above analogy in mind there clearly are, as research and the study of the three principals mentioned above indicate, behaviors good principals engage in which have a high probability of positively influencing the culture of our schools. Understanding these behaviors and working on their exhibition is a necessary first step toward creating positive cultures. While some of them are easy to exhibit in different circumstances, they may present real challenges. However, they are worthy behaviors, and principals concerned with positively impacting their school's culture ought to seriously examine the way in which they are engaging or failing to engage in them on a regular basis.

TEN KEY PRINCIPAL BEHAVIORS

Summarized and enumerated below are 10 key behaviors that principals ought to adopt in order to create a more positive culture. These behaviors, though grounded in research, are presented and intended to be ready to emulate.

1. **Be visible to all school stakeholders.**

   Research and sound practice have proven that school leaders who are visible to stakeholders help create and foster positive school cultures (Fiore, 1999). This is largely due to the overwhelming sense of comfort reported when the principal is visible regularly and in various settings. In addition, visibility, exhibited through such behaviors as Management by Walking Around, makes the management tasks of school leaders more efficient (Frase & Melton, 1992). It takes little more than a strong commitment to push aside management tasks and leave the office at key times throughout the day.

2. **Communicate regularly and purposefully.**

   Effective communication must occur in good times, as well as in bad times. If the principal is known to communicate with students, staff members, and parents only when there are problems, then there will be a negative impact felt on the culture of the school. The best school leaders use varied forms of communication to regularly provide feedback to all stakeholders. The principal's understanding of the importance of visibility makes this easier and more natural.

3. **Never forget that principals are role models.**

   Less effective administrators fail to see themselves as role models (Fiore, 1999). They mistakenly believe that teachers are viewed as role models, while missing the point that many members of a school community see principals in that capacity (Foriska, 1994). Principals must be aware that they are the most influential people in a school system. Teachers, staff, parents, students, and community members *do* look to the school leaders as role models. With this in mind, principals should model behaviors consistent with the sustenance of a positive school culture.

4. **Be passionate about your work.**

   The most effective school leaders seem to love the work they are engaged in. They have a passion for schools and a passion for leadership that their followers can clearly witness. The imperative for all school leaders is to become more passionate about their work and clearer about what they hope to accomplish (Greenfield, 1985). This may be a difficult one, for passion comes from within and is difficult to copy.

5. **Understand how responsible you are for the culture.**

   The best school leaders believe that they are responsible for virtually everything that happens in their schools. Rather than bemoaning this, these leaders welcome the responsibility and use it for the betterment of education. The most effective principals realize their responsibility to protect the needs and integrity of the entire school community (Sergiovanni, 1996). They do not "pass the buck" and blame others for problems in the school. These principals are highly proactive leaders.

6. **Keep yourself organized.**

   School administrators who are organized find time management to be much less burdensome than do disorganized administrators. This gives them more time for instructional leadership, school-community relations, and personnel management. Studies have shown (Whitaker, 1997; Fiore, 1999) that stakeholders appreciate and rely on the organization of their leader. If organization is not an inherent strength of the principal, then the principal must have office staff who can assist in this regard. In other words, this is a weakness that must be managed.

7. **Exhibit a positive outlook.**

As role models, the best school administrators realize that attitudes are, indeed, contagious. To create and sustain a positive school culture, school leaders must consistently radiate positive energies. They must proactively approach their work, never forgetting the mission of the school. Furthermore, effective principals strengthen the culture of their school by ensuring that its mission and vision are shared by the entire school community (Buell, 1992).

8. **Take pride in the physical appearance of your schools.**

With estimates that 65 to 80 percent of households do not have children in our schools, school leaders must realize that the physical appearance of their schools is the only aspect of which most of the public is aware. Therefore, effective leaders recognize the importance of always making sure their school looks as neat and attractive as possible. More significantly, they do not leave this to chance, relying on custodial staff and maintenance staff members to perform this task. Effective leaders, instead, take responsibility themselves for ensuring that their buildings are neat and attractive.

9. **Empower others appropriately.**

The leaders needed in our schools understand when and how to empower others to share leadership. They realize that people need a stake in the outcome of an event and the capacity to lead before they can be empowered. They are aware that "empowerment enables; it does not simply permit" (Schlechty, 1997). They appropriately empower teachers, support staff, students, and parents.

10. **Demonstrate stewardship.**

School leaders who understand their roles as stewards of the community are inspiring to followers. Effective administrators exercise stewardship when they commit themselves to serving, caring for, and protecting their schools and their stakeholders (Sergiovanni, 1996). Principals need to make the choice to serve their school first. Without making such a choice, a leader's capacity to lead is profoundly limited (Greenleaf, 1977).

Reducing and simplifying the lessons learned from some of the country's best principals obviously does not allow readers to reap all of the benefits derived from a study of their effectiveness. At the same time, the 10 items above really do effectively summarize the beliefs and exhibited behaviors of these principals. The challenge for all school leaders is to internalize this list. By doing that and by paying attention to your own positive behaviors, you can have a tremendous, lasting impact on the culture of your school.

There clearly are other roadblocks principals will face on the path to creating positive cultures. An obvious one involves the difficulty of getting stakeholder groups with different understandings (i.e., parents and teachers) to agree on methodology in all cases. This need not and should not be the exclusive task of leadership, though. Great leaders lead people to a common set of beliefs or mission. The leaders needed for our schools work hard at creating and sustaining a schoolwide mission that focuses on students and their achievement. When the enumerated behaviors above are internalized and, consequently, exhibited, school stakeholders come to rely on the principal's consistency in light of this mission, or combination of core beliefs. Issues of methodology become more difficult to debate when decisions are grounded in a vision, mission, or set of beliefs that everybody shares and is bound to.

A second apparent roadblock involves the potential time commitment inherent in changing behaviors. In recognition of that understanding, I offer this opinion. If, in fact, the ten key behaviors explained in this chapter will require you to make radical changes, thus committing inordinate amounts of time, consider the time savings that these behaviors will give you in the long run. Remaining organized and empowering others, for example, will certainly pay huge and obvious dividends in the long run. The time spent working on these behaviors will undoubtedly be returned to you once the behaviors have become habits.

Now, what happens if principals choose not to work on these behaviors? Does this guarantee that the school culture will become negative? While a guarantee cannot be made, there are principal leadership behaviors, which have been consistently shown to have a negative impact on school culture. These behaviors should be examined, and principals should work to ensure that they rarely exhibit them in their schools. Enumerated below, these statements characterize some of the more prevalent behaviors of principals in schools with negative cultures.

- Principals of schools with negative cultures are rarely seen outside of the office.
- Principals of schools with negative cultures find little time for communication, particularly in written form.
- Principals of schools with negative cultures feel that other people are responsible for their school building's physical needs. They take much more passive roles in decorating and furnishing their schools.
- Principals of schools with negative cultures see themselves as the lone leader, or "boss" of the school. As such, they never empower teachers to lead.

- ♦ Principals of schools with negative cultures are poorly organized.

- ♦ Principals of schools with negative cultures habitually make excuses for their schools' shortcomings, blaming inadequacies on outside influences.

These six items do not characterize all of the behaviors exhibited by principals who negatively impact school culture. Instead, they represent themes that are rather consistently seen in schools perceived by stakeholders to have negative cultures. The question, which needs to be asked here, is this: Are any of these themes, after honest introspection, present in your school? To cause deep concern, these themes must be present more often than they are absent. If, for example, you find yourself feeling disorganized from time to time, I would not be so quick to call disorganization a theme. If, on the other hand, you do recognize that you are habitually making excuses or blaming others for problems in your school, then this reactive behavior should be considered a theme.

When such themes are present in our schools, they have a lasting impact on all constituents. Teachers, as an example, begin blaming others, and failing to regularly communicate, when they see the principal consistently modeling such behaviors. Parents stay away, or put more accurately, hide when visibility and accessibility are not modeled and/or valued by the principal. This, it is significant to remember, does not mean that parents become less critical. In fact, the reverse effect is generally noticed. In a nutshell, school principals who find themselves wondering how they can positively influence the culture of their schools must closely examine, internalize, and genuinely exhibit the ten key behaviors outlined earlier in this chapter. By the same token, they must recognize when some of the more negative themes outlined are present in their schools. Subsequently, they must work diligently to eliminate them.

One final note for this chapter. While I do believe that teachers are the most important adults in a school, a point I will elaborate on in the next chapter, I also believe that the principal is unquestionably the most influential. All principals, whether relishing in the power of that statement or not, must recognize the responsibility that comes with having such a high degree of influence. Similarly, principals must never forget that their behaviors can readily influence a school's culture and move it in a more positive direction. The behaviors of the principal really are the key, and these behaviors must be carefully measured to insure that we create the kinds of positive schools our children need and deserve. Their exhibition, joined with perseverance, will lead to the creation of a positive school culture or the sustenance of an already existing positive one.

SUMMARY OF KEY POINTS

♦ The key to a positive culture rests firmly in the hands of the principal.

♦ There clearly are behaviors good principals engage in, which have a high probability of positively influencing the culture of our schools.

♦ School principals who find themselves wondering how they can positively influence the culture of their schools must closely examine, internalize, and genuinely exhibit the 10 key behaviors outlined earlier in this chapter.

♦ The principal is unquestionably the most influential adult in a school.

4

RECOGNIZING AND UTILIZING TEACHER LEADERS: PIONEERING A CULTURAL REVOLUTION

As we all know, teachers come in many forms and wear many faces. Some see their job solely as "deliverer of content" while others take a more nurturing, child-centered approach to their craft. The latter understand that they are not called to simply pour knowledge into otherwise empty children but, instead, are there to foster the development of the whole child. In many ways, the power teachers have over students is immense, and their influence over students' attitudes, beliefs, self-concept, and achievement is more monumental and immediate than the influence of any other individual in the school. As such, teachers, in many ways, shape the way students feel about school. Within the confines of the classroom, the teacher is the main determinant of the culture. Their behavior sets the tone and provides the foundation for what children do and how they feel about what they do. Within the larger boundaries of the school building, the teacher is an important player in advancing or blocking a schoolwide culture from being fostered. They have the ability to be a team player or the Lone Ranger, a builder of positive culture or a blocker of positive culture. The most effective school principals are the ones who understand this teacher power and welcome teacher leaders as builders and brokers of a positive school culture. It is these principals who recognize and utilize teacher leaders, thus pioneering a cultural revolution.

THE CLASSROOM IS THE KEY

"Teachers' classroom leadership is the real center of meaningful school change. Only in the classroom can teachers create more and higher learning for students" (Kaplan & Evans, 1997, p. 5). This is why I have always maintained that, while the principal is the most influential person in the school, the teachers are the most important. This is also why it is patently illogical for school leaders desirous of building positive cultures to fail to bring teachers into their plans at the onset. Instead, as I have indicated, the most effective principals are those who utilize teachers' leadership skills in the creation of a positive schoolwide culture and then assist their teachers in fostering the same type of cultural development in their own class-rooms. I maintain that a school cannot be changed and im-proved until such transformational plans are introduced and advanced at the classroom level. This is easier when principals regularly and purposefully communicate with teachers and are consequently viewed by them as being highly visible. A principal cannot be connected to the classroom culture unless the principal is first regularly seen as a stakeholder in it. By in-volving teachers in the creation of schoolwide cultures, princi-pals should want and expect reciprocal involvement in class-room cultures. A key ingredient of the savvy principal's suc-cess lies in the principal's ability to regularly become involved in classroom activities.

In further thinking about positive classroom cultures, I cannot help but think back to so many of the classroom envi-ronments I have witnessed and experienced. I think first of the many physical characteristics of these classrooms. Most nota-bly, as my mind wanders back, I am reminded of some of the encouraging, inspirational messages I have seen displayed, and I begin to wonder if they were mere decorations or strong declarations of what the teachers in these classrooms really be-lieved. I further see in my mind the energy and enthusiasm that emanates from these more positive classroom environ-ments, and I cannot help but more clearly understand the power teachers possess. Along this line, there is a short decla-ration by child psychologist, Haim Ginott, posted in many classrooms throughout the country, which states:

> I've come to the frightening conclusion that I am the decisive element in the classroom. It's my per-sonal approach that creates the climate. It's my daily mood that makes the weather. As a teacher, I possess a tremendous power to make a child's life miserable or joyous. I can be a tool of torture or an

instrument of inspiration. I can humiliate or humor, hurt or heal. In all situations, it is my response that decides whether a crisis will be escalated or de-escalated and a child humanized or dehumanized.

In light of Ginott's words, the importance of teachers as creators of classroom climates cannot be ignored. Thinking back to the iceberg analogy from Chapter 1, we are aware that a positive climate needs to rest on the solid foundation of a positive culture if it is to have any lasting effects. As the decisive element in the classroom, the teacher assumes a role similar to the role of the principal in relation to the entire school. As such, many of the same behaviors that principals engage in to improve the culture of their schools are appropriately modified for use by classroom teachers. For, as we know, culture is the foundation upon which climate rests. It is in the creation of these cultures that teachers become decisive elements. Think back, if you will, to the list of 10 key principal leadership behaviors in Chapter 3. Stated in terms of the teacher's role in their classroom, they would look something like this:

1. **Be visible and accessible to students and parents.**

    When students feel that they have access to the teacher, they are more likely to feel a sense of security. A visible, accessible teacher communicates to students that they are approachable. Additionally, parents feel secure knowing that they too, have access to the teacher. With many parents feeling intimidated by teachers (Riley, 1994), it becomes vitally important for teachers to extend the open hand. Being visible and accessible is one way of doing this.

2. **Communicate regularly and purposefully.**

    Effective communication must occur in good times, as well as in bad times. If the teacher is known to communicate with students and parents only when there are problems, there will be a negative impact felt on the culture of the classroom. Students will quickly learn to fear teacher comments and parents will feel anxiety any time the teacher calls or sends a note home. The best teachers use varied forms of communication and regularly provide feedback to students and parents alike. Because of this, they can be depended on to give honest, unbiased feedback and assessment.

3. **Never forget that you are a role model.**

Students, in many cases, spend more time with their teachers than with any other adults. Therefore, the behaviors modeled by teachers are often the most reliable and enduring adult behaviors modeled for students. To create a positive school culture, teachers must be aware that their behaviors become the model behaviors students observe and, ultimately copy. A positive attitude is contagious and infectious.

4. **Be passionate about your teaching.**

The most effective teachers seem to love the work that they are engaged in. They have a passion for children and a passion for teaching that children and parents can clearly witness. The imperative for all school staff, therefore, is to become more passionate about their work and clearer about what they hope to accomplish (Greenfield, 1985). This, as mentioned in the leadership context, may be a difficult one, for passion comes from within and is difficult to copy. Teachers who are passionate about their work have a much better chance of transferring this passion to students than do less passionate, unmotivated teachers.

5. **Understand how responsible you are for the culture in your classroom.**

The best school leaders and teachers believe that they are responsible for virtually everything that happens in their schools or in their classrooms. Rather than bemoaning this, these teachers and leaders welcome the responsibility, and use it for the betterment of education. The most effective teachers recognize their power in the classroom, in terms of creating a climate conducive to student learning and risk-taking (Ginott, 1972). Understanding this responsibility, they ensure that their classrooms have underlying cultures, which enable student success. They recognize that students have a significant role in this, but that they are chiefly responsible for fostering these classroom cultures.

6. **Keep yourself organized.**

   Teachers who are organized find that time management is less burdensome than do disorganized teachers. This creates a less frantic classroom atmosphere and allows for more time to effectively and genuinely communicate with students and parents. Additionally, it models the value of organization to students, which, in turn, allows them to be more successful. Studies have shown (Whitaker, 1997; Fiore, 1999) that stakeholders appreciate and rely on the organization of their leader. If organization is not an inherent strength of the teacher, then they must pay increased attention to this. In other words, this is a weakness that must be managed.

7. **Demonstrate a positive attitude.**

   "I want my students, wherever I teach, to feel part of a compassionate learning community where they are honored as individuals, where they respect each other, and where they respect and love learning itself." (Kohl, 1998, p. 18) These words exemplify the kind of positive attitude teachers need. Having a deep respect for learning and a love for students sets the foundation for a positive classroom attitude. When teachers exhibit these positive attitudes, they are, indeed, contagious. To create and sustain a positive classroom culture, teachers must consistently radiate positive energies. They must proactively approach their work, never forgetting the mission of the school.

8. **Take pride in the physical, child-centered appearance of your classroom.**

   People, we know, often do judge books by their covers. As such, a child-centered classroom gives a positive outward appearance to parents and community members. More importantly, the display of student work gives children a sense of worth and allows all to see the value of their accomplishments. The display of student work demonstrates an attitude to students that their work is valuable and important. Classrooms in which no student work is displayed demonstrate less friendly environments (DeLeon & Medina, 1997). A positive culture is, in many ways, reflected in the physical appearance of the classroom.

9. **Empower students and give them responsibility.**

   The best teachers understand when and how to empower their students and give them responsibility. They realize that students need to understand the stake they have in their own learning. These teachers understand that students must be assisted in connecting what they are learning to their own lives. When students recognize this, they become more willing to assume responsibility. These teachers are also aware that "empowerment enables; it does not simply permit" (Schlechty, 1997). As such, they become enablers of student growth and learning.

10. **Demonstrate stewardship.**

    Teachers who understand their roles as stewards of the classroom community are inspiring to students. The most effective teachers, just like the

most effective administrators, exercise stewardship when they commit themselves to serving,
caring for, and protecting their schools and their
stakeholders (Sergiovanni, 1996). Teachers need
to make the choice to serve their students before
having their students serve them. Without making such a choice, a leader's capacity to lead is
profoundly limited (Greenleaf, 1977).

I have had the distinct pleasure of working with many
teachers who have embodied these ten behaviors. Perhaps
you have as well. However, it must be noted that even when
all of these behaviors are not present all of the time, a positive
culture can still exist. These behaviors represent the ideal.
They illustrate for us the beliefs and behaviors that we want
teachers to regularly exhibit. Positive school leadership ought
to reinforce these behaviors. This leadership needs to model
appropriate behaviors in order that they become easily understood by all. For this reason, there is a strong relationship between these 10 behaviors and the ten principal behaviors from
Chapter 3.

THE TEACHER AS LEADER

We have looked at the teacher's role in creating, fostering,
and sustaining a positive culture within the confines of their
classroom. As discussed, this role is arguably the most important role in students' school lives. When teachers allow positive classroom cultures to flourish, students have more positive attitudes about school. This, in turn, leads to increased
achievement for all. As the saying goes, "It is your attitude,
not your aptitude, which determines your altitude." Teachers,
through their daily interactions with their students, have the
greatest impact on student attitudes.

In examining schoolwide culture, however, the teacher
plays an unmistakable and also significant role. Teachers can
severely hamper, or in some cases prevent the efforts of even
the most successful principals to advance a positive culture or
they can be the principal's greatest allies. Think, as an example, of your school faculty for a moment. In your mind, please

create a mental image of the last faculty meeting you had. As studies have shown (Whitaker, 1997; Fiore, 1999), faculty meetings are a valued part of a positive school's culture. In fact, teachers in positive schools look forward to them. However, the opposite is also true. In schools with more negative cultures, teachers tend to dread faculty meetings and see them as unproductive. Why? Part of it has to do with the group dynamics in these schools, as I will explain. More of it, as you will see, has to do with the ways in which the principal allows these group dynamics to manifest themselves.

In this mental image you have created, think specifically of where faculty members sit. In most typical schools, the more negative teachers tend to congregate together in the back of the room. The result of this arrangement is often an uncomfortable, unproductive meeting for the positive teachers and the principal (Whitaker, 1999). The group of negative members makes snide comments and exhibits body language that is often intimidating. In this way, a single group of teachers, often not a large one, can have a profoundly negative impact on an element that is otherwise a strong component of positive school cultures. They effectively block the principal's efforts in creating a positive culture. By merely altering the way in which the room is arranged for the meeting, the principal can disempower the negative teachers. This can be done in a variety of ways. The savvy principal may remove the back tables, or fill them with handouts and/or refreshments. Similarly, the principal may assign people to sit in specific groups. The principal may arrange the room so all staff members are seated in a circle. Also, the principal may choose to intentionally position a positive leader (i.e., an assistant principal) right in the middle of the negative group. While I strongly believe that principals should empower teachers when appropriate, they cannot allow themselves to continue empowering the negative ones. Instead, power must swiftly be removed from these people and be restored to the positive teachers.

Many people may regard the above statement as being much easier said than done. However, great school leaders know that there are ways to disempower negative staff members. Todd Whitaker (1999) explains specific methods for doing so in *Dealing with Difficult Teachers*. The most important step is to make negative staff members feel uncomfortable. While this may appear, at first, to be a statement lacking compassion, it really is not when you consider the alternative. If the most negative members of your teaching staff feel comfortable all of the time, it probably means that the more positive staff members do not. Keep in mind that many negative staff members lack the interpersonal intelligence to even begin to realize the effect their negativity has on other people.

Consider the faculty meeting you pictured before. As negative staff members snidely make comments designed to inhibit risk-taking or growth, the more positive staff members become afraid, or at least unwilling, to share a positive thought or to agree with a positive idea. They, and perhaps the principal, are the most uncomfortable people in the room. It really should not be this way. If somebody needs to be made uncomfortable, then let it be the negative people. They are the staff members most in need of being disempowered.

Again, whether we are talking about a staff meeting or any other gathering, this can be done in several ways. Among the methods to use are: empowering positive staff members, raising difficult teachers' interpersonal intelligence level, using approaches at faculty meetings which physically separate the negative people, reducing negativity in the teachers' workroom, making teachers accept responsibility for their negativity and the situations which result from this negativity, and using peers to help make the difficult members feel more uncomfortable (Whitaker, 1999). Principals need to remember that negative staff members have been the way they currently are for a very long time. It has become comfortable for them to be this way. The only hope of changing these individuals lies in the leader's ability to swiftly stop making negativity so comfortable for them.

GIVING TEACHERS RESPONSIBILITY

The teacher's role is seen as being even more influential in schools that practice some form of participatory management, or site-based decision making. In these environments, teachers are naturally more involved in the governance of the school. As such, it is easy to see how important it is for there to be congruence between what teachers believe and how they behave and the beliefs and behaviors of the principal. With this notion in mind, consider the importance of both the hiring process and the staff development process. These are key times for principals to ascertain the extent to which stakeholders' beliefs are compatible with each other. The best principals constantly work on molding the beliefs of teachers, from the moment they are interviewed and throughout their tenure. This is done to ensure that there is congruence in beliefs between them. It is done to ensure that the mission statement reflects their beliefs, and thus has meaning. Not everything needs to be viewed harmoniously, but the major beliefs regarding education and the treatment of students must be consistent within and among faculty members. When such congruence exists, barriers and divisions in relationships tend to break down. This, in turn, makes it easier for groups to make decisions and reach consensus. This is made possible largely because of how well individual group members know, trust, and respect one another. The result is a culture much like that described by David Bohm (1996, pp. 16–17) in the following illustration:

> From time to time, (the) tribe (gathered) in a circle. They just talked and talked and talked, apparently to no purpose. They made no decisions. There was no leader. And everybody could participate. There may have been wise men or wise women who were listened to a bit more—the older ones—but everybody could talk. The meeting went on, until finally it seemed to stop for no reason at all and the group dispersed. Yet after that, everybody seemed to know what to do, because they understood each other so well. Then they could get together in smaller groups and do something or decide things.

The dialogue described in this passage is the type of dialogue characteristic of the strong communication that exists in high functioning groups. When people share a common culture; that is, when they are inspired by the same mission, envision the same outcomes for students, and have participated in many of the same rituals, traditions, and ceremonies, then there exists an almost subconscious level of understanding between them. Schools in which the common culture is strong find communication among and between constituents to flow naturally and effortlessly, much like in the tribe described by Bohm. Think about your own school again. Do conversations flow easily when groups of people are standing around the copy machine or the coffeepot? On the other hand, is there a lot of whispering at these locales? This tells you something about whether or not the culture of your school is as it is in Bohm's example. When such a culture is not present and people are not open and trusting with one another, then communication takes the form of a much more conscious, measured dialogue. Messages run the risk of getting lost as people search for the right way to articulate things. Energy becomes wasted and not clearly focused in these organizations.

Therefore, school leadership in its broadest sense must include some variation of the use of teachers as leaders. When it does, then school principals are sending a message that they trust the teachers to lead when it is appropriate. As a result, there is not as much division of labor as there would be in a classically bureaucratic organization. Furthermore, using teachers as leaders can be instrumental in helping the principal to open up the level of trust that exists within the school. If I, for example, am trusting of you, will you not often become more trusting of me? If you answered "Yes" to that question, then does it not stand to reason that teachers who are trusted to lead will also feel the same way?

This does not mean that principals need to use shared governance all the time and with all decisions that face them. To do so, as your own practical experience has probably shown you, would often be counterproductive. It does mean, however, that leaders who empower their teachers to lead when appropriate find a common understanding between themselves and teachers to be present far more often than do principals who believe in strictly adhering to clearly defined roles and responsibilities. This "division of labor" mindset leads to a collection of individuals who understand their roles and responsibilities but fail to see the connection between themselves and others. This is significant, for it is these connections that so strongly assist in creating the common culture in a school. The more connections we can create and the more aware we can make others of schoolwide roles and responsibilities the stronger and more positive we will make the school culture. Principals must recognize that shared governance gives people a stake in decisions and naturally draws them into common understandings and beliefs.

BUILDING THE
TEACHER/STUDENT RELATIONSHIP

Of paramount importance to the teachers' role in creating, fostering, and sustaining a positive school culture is the quality of the relationships they build with their students. Teachers who create great distance between themselves and their students make it exceedingly difficult for students to develop relationships with them. Their distance is often interpreted by students as a barrier or a wall that clearly puts students and teachers into different castes. As such, students may begin to develop their own group culture, but it will often become one that is incongruent with the adult culture in the school building.

This is not to say that a teacher's primary responsibility ought to be on developing relationships with students. Obviously, there is a science to the craft of teaching that must be understood, consistently reexamined, and perfected anew with each student. We are, as I have said, deep within an age of accountability. Teaching, or more importantly, learning must be at the center of our schools' existence. However, the relationships that teachers develop with students have a direct impact on the teacher's ability to teach and the students' ability to learn. For this reason, these relationships must be deemed vitally important.

I, like most of you, have worked with difficult students who I really didn't enjoy being with. In my best, more rational moments I understand that this was often not the student's fault. Nevertheless, if I am to be brutally honest, I must admit that there are a few students I have worked with who I simply did not get along with. Though my professional pride sometimes refuses to acknowledge this, I must say that these students did not learn as much from me as did the vast majority of students who I genuinely loved and shared mutual respect with. Though I tried my best to teach them, I know that our relationship may have erected a wall that was not conducive to learning. Think of the negative impact a teacher can have if they discover a misunderstanding, or in the worse cases a dislike, between themselves and the majority of the students they work with. Not only can this negative teacher harm the school building culture, but they will certainly prevent a positive culture from developing in the classroom due to the distance that is created by not having positive relationships with students.

Principals often mistakenly assume that all skilled teachers know how to develop positive relationships with students. This assumption is simply not true. Many teachers, even those skilled in their craft, need to be taught about the benefits of being positive with children. They need to be assisted in understanding how important it is to increase their levels of praise for students, while decreasing their levels of criticism. They need to be encouraged to cheerfully greet students in the morning and to informally show genuine interest in their students' lives. They need to realize that a blanket condemnation of Pokemon, rock music, or whatever the craze of the day is, only perpetuates a feeling among students of disconnectedness with teachers. I admit that I do not understand the attraction to Pokemon cards. I do realize, however, that knowing who Pikachu is would be essential knowledge for me if I still worked in an elementary school.

It is not important for teachers to fully accept and embrace all that makes up the modern popular culture our students are a part of. In fact, doing so may be counterproductive. Students need to see teachers as role models and as examples of responsible adults. What teachers do need to do, to best build relationships with students, is to demonstrate at least a minimal understanding of the students' world. As Stephen Covey says, the most effective people are those who "seek first to understand, then to be understood" (Covey, 1989). Understanding of students' interests, in this regard, is probably more important than acceptance.

As a principal, I always required my staff members to be in the hall, greeting children at the start of each school day. I further required that they take similar poses as the students were leaving at the conclusion of the school day. I firmly believe that it is vitally important for students to receive an enthusiastic personal greeting and farewell each and every school day. I cannot control the environment that students leave before they come to school. Likewise, I have no influence on the environment that they return to at the conclusion of the day. Therefore, I insist that all students begin and end their days in school with a smile and a positive, personal greeting. Not only does it set the stage for a positive day, but it also shows genuine caring on the part of the entire school staff. It illustrates for students that they are important and that their presence each day is of value.

The same beliefs and principles hold true for teacher behaviors that occur within the confines of the classroom. Whenever possible, the best teachers try to make their lessons relevant to the world students live in. They assign writing assignments around topics of interest to children. They provide literature for children, which delivers an important life lesson, but does so within a context that children will enjoy and understand. They craft mathematics problems around items that are popular with the students, and that students can relate to. They do many more things, but they do them all with the knowledge that the best learning takes place when it is relevant and connected. A natural by-product is that these teacher behaviors demonstrate an understanding of the students' interests. The teachers, in turn, are viewed by the students as being pretty "cool" and more approachable. This tears down barriers and helps to build positive relationships.

Teachers further create positive relationships, thereby fostering a positive culture, when they correct children's behavior in a less punitive manner. I believe that schools should be places of discipline, but I can never support teachers yelling at, or otherwise belittling, students. I have always insisted that we correct "misbehaviors," we do not correct "bad children." The best teachers are those who recognize that behavior is a choice. As such, when students make a bad choice and misbehave, great teachers let the students know that they regret the bad choice, they administer the consequences, and they explain what will happen if the student makes a similar choice in the future. Likewise, these teachers reward students for appropriate choices.

Within this framework, we can be very demanding in the behaviors we expect and tolerate from our students. This is, by no means, "soft discipline." I, like many of you, have suspended students, removed desired privileges like trips and assemblies, contacted hundreds of parents, and engaged in many other behavior-correcting techniques. The importance is that I always did so in a manner that clearly informed the student that *they* chose the behavior, the consequence was a result of *their* behavior, and that more drastic measures would happen if *they* chose to repeat the misbehavior. I did not yell or demean the student in any way. My goal was to teach students how to behave, and to do it purposefully, yet compassionately.

When teachers take the time to understand students, when they intentionally show that they understand students, and when they engage in management techniques that are firm, yet compassionate, then they are taking important steps toward developing appropriate, positive relationships with students. The impact this can have on the school's culture is significant. Children really do not care how much you know until they know how much you care. Our schools need teachers who truly care about children, and who are not afraid to show that this is so.

For these reasons, whether the principal is wise enough to empower teachers or not, teachers are leaders. They lead their classrooms, and they create and sustain their classroom cultures on a regular basis. If teachers are included in the creation of a schoolwide culture, if they are given formal leadership responsibilities when appropriate, and if they are assisted in being compassionate and understanding of students' lives, then they are well on their way to pioneering a cultural revolution in our schools. Teachers are simply far too important to be left out as we create positive school cultures in which all of our students can learn.

SUMMARY OF KEY POINTS

♦ The most effective principals are those who utilize teachers' leadership skills in the creation of a positive schoolwide culture and then assist their teachers in fostering the same type of cultural development in their own classrooms.

♦ Many of the same behaviors principals engage in to improve the culture of their schools are appropriately modified for use by classroom teachers.

♦ Teachers can severely hamper, or in some cases prevent the efforts of even the most successful principals to advance a positive culture or they can be the principal's greatest allies.

♦ School leadership in its broadest sense must include some variation of the use of teachers as leaders.

♦ Of paramount importance to the teachers' role in creating, fostering, and sustaining a positive school culture is the quality of the relationships they build with their students.

5

EMBRACING YOUR MOST POWERFUL STAKEHOLDERS: PARENTS

As more and more people begin to understand the powerful role parents play in their children's education, all schools must look closely at the ways in which they attempt to keep this vital constituent group welcomed and involved. In actuality, the concept of parental involvement being beneficial to students is easy to understand and logical to accept. The more difficult part is answering the question, "How"? How do schools appropriately involve parents? What are the real benefits of parents as vital, accepted members of a school's culture?

Virtually all of our nation's schools struggle, to some degree, with parental involvement issues. For some, the concern centers on a seeming inability to involve parents. Other schools experience a high degree of parent interest and attendance at relevant functions, but have a more challenging time trying to figure out what to do with the parents. Still, others utilize parents with some degree of regularity, but find themselves unsure about the benefits, if any, that such parent utilization has for their schools. In this chapter, I address these issues and frame them in the context of cultural improvement. That is to say, this chapter will assist you in understanding parental involvement issues from the framework of school culture, while also illustrating the improvements possible by school leaders effectively utilizing these invaluable stakeholders.

CONTEMPORARY PARENTS: A SNAPSHOT

The mere mention of parental involvement's significance causes some educators to bristle in defense. These well-intentioned teachers and administrators argue that parents either choose to involve themselves in their children's schools out of nosiness or distrust, or they simply claim to be too busy to involve themselves at all. Many of these educators maintain that their school does all it can to utilize parents, but to no avail. The problem, these individuals continuously insist, is with the parents themselves. To assist this group of educators in understanding parental motives and to help them align these motives with their own, thus enabling parents to become an integral part of the school's culture, a snapshot of contemporary parents must be examined. Through careful consideration of this snapshot, I hope both an understanding of and an appreciation for contemporary parents are inevitable. It is important to note that this snapshot is, in no way, an attempt to pass judgement on any parents. In fact, many of the changes witnessed in family structure have been beneficial, both to children and to the larger society. The next few paragraphs, instead, are meant to merely provide a snapshot, or quick picture, for those who may not otherwise stop to realize that parents of today are, in many ways, different from those of days gone by.

One does not need to be a "researcher" to see the changes in family dynamics that our culture has experienced. Among the most notable of these dynamics is the employment of the working mother. More and more, we see mothers of school-aged children pursuing careers or seeking full-time employment out of economic necessity. Consider that in 1940 fewer than 9 percent of all women with children worked outside the home (U.S. Bureau of Labor Statistics, 1987). In 1997, by comparison, the U.S. Bureau of Labor Statistics reported that 76.5 percent of women with children between the ages of 6 and 13 were in the labor force.

There are several factors that have led to this societal shift. Among them are inflation, the increased cost of child rearing, and the decreased likelihood of living the "American Dream" on a single income (Procidano & Fisher, 1992). Also contributing are two other significant factors; the substantial increase in the United State's divorce rate and the growing percentage of women giving birth out of wedlock. In fact, while widowhood was once the primary cause of one-parent families, recent statistics indicate that 85 percent of single-parent homes result from separation or divorce (The National Data Book, 1998).

The apparent depreciation of fatherhood that these statistics suggest, as all educators can attest to, creates real problems for our schools and society. Just ask any teacher, administrator, or other school employee what they think the effects of fatherless homes are on students. They could tell you, and research confirms, that children from fatherless homes are often less productive in school and responsible for a high percentage of criminal behavior (Blankenhorn, 1995). Also and rather obviously, when there is only one parent providing care for a child, one would expect a reduction in the family's ability to be involved in that child's school. Logic indicates the reduction in this ability would be approximately 50 percent.

In addition to these dramatic changes in family configurations, the relative wealth of American households has also experienced significant changes during the last half-century. Consider that in 1996, 14.5 million American children under the age of 18 lived in poverty (The National Data Book, 1998). These children attend our schools, and for obvious reasons they often do so with little involvement from their parents.

There is much more that could be said regarding this small, and sometimes blurry, snapshot. In order to be crystal clear, it would have needed to be a montage or a scrapbook so it could truly capture the diversity. For our purposes, however, the above snapshot provides us with some necessary information as we attempt to discover what life is like for many of our parents, and then what to do to make these parents an integral part of our school's culture.

It is also worth mentioning that this snapshot obviously does not describe a great many of our school's parents. Again, doing so would require us to transform the snapshot into a scrapbook. However, though many are not described by the statistical information I have given you, they are absolutely affected by it. This is so because of the impact the information stated earlier has on society as a whole. One does not need to be a genius, for example, to see the larger societal impact of working parents and single-parent households. Even if such things do not directly affect me, they do affect my school community and the decisions it makes. Parent-Teacher organizations, Open House schedules, and a host of other schoolwide events have their scheduling, their format, and their expectations shaped by these societal profiles. For example, while it once may have been acceptable to schedule school events for parents in the afternoon, such practices are often doomed for failure today. Instead, in recognition of parental responsibilities, most schools schedule such events in the evening, to allow for maximum parental involvement.

PARENTAL INVOLVEMENT
AND STUDENT ACHIEVEMENT

Though the National PTA considers parental involvement to be of vital importance to student success, does this organization's opinion make it necessarily so? To answer this, consider what scores of studies regarding school effectiveness have discovered: student achievement and overall school performance are intertwined with parent involvement (Levine and Lezotte, 1990). As the following figure illustrates, when parents are strongly linked with a school's culture, that is when their involvement is regular, ordinary, and expected, student achievement can be profoundly affected.

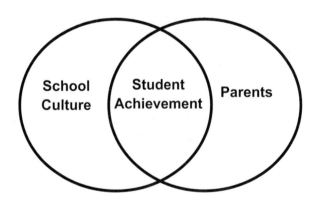

For parents to become integral parts of positive school cultures, it is of paramount importance that they instill in their children the sense that school is vitally important. Schools, on the other hand, need to understand the importance of parents and must work hard to understand parents' perspectives. When these two ideas are put into practice parents become integral parts of a school's culture. We already know that healthy, positive school cultures are linked with increased student achievement, the underlying purpose of our schools. Inviting, or rather insisting, that parents are important components of these cultures adds an often missing dimension to student success.

Developing and maintaining healthy relationships with parents is, therefore, vitally important to the success of any school. These healthy relationships, in which parents understand their roles in relation to the school's mission, come about through involvement and engagement of all parents. They do not come about in schools that alienate parents or fail to include them in the very development and nurturing of the school's overall mission. Here are three simple reasons why these healthy relationships are so important in the creation of positive school cultures:

1. Students are more successful in school when their parents and school personnel work closely and cooperatively.

2. Parents will be more supportive and willing to give educators the benefit of the doubt, even in stress-filled and emotional encounters, when there is a history of working together.

3. Everyone in the schooling business (parents, teachers, administrators, and students) will benefit from two-way information sharing and collaborative problem solving. (McEwan, 1998, p. 79)

To further involve parents in a manner that would directly impact student achievement, it is necessary for school leaders to include them in the development, articulation, and continuous revision of the school's mission statement. Doing so enables parents to accurately comprehend what the school stakeholders believe in. This point, though restated in virtually every chapter of this book, cannot be overstated, and must be accepted. Parents, like all other stakeholder groups, are much more effective allies when they completely understand what our schools are all about. This is made far easier when the behavior of all adults in our schools reflects the stated mission. Involving parents in the revision of these statements gives them ownership, which we know increases the likelihood that they will abide by, believe in, and articulate, through their behaviors, all that the mission statement espouses. Creating the level of parental involvement I am speaking of is often best accomplished through the creation of Parent Advisory Boards and the inclusion of parents in all committees on which they have a stake. Specific roles of such committees will be discussed further on in this chapter.

Educators, particularly educational leaders, are inundated with requests or mandates that stakeholders be involved in decision making within their schools. These cries for involvement, though correct in many respects, fall on deaf ears in many instances because some school leaders are unaware of how to share decision-making in an appropriate manner. There is a misconception that all decisions need to be made by a committee. There is a further misconception that all stakeholders want to be involved in decisions. Still a third misconception postulates that shared decision-making automatically leads to increased acceptance of the results of a decision. Applying these misconceptions often leads principals and teachers to frustration because they find out that in some instances stakeholders simply want the decision made for them.

So, how does a leader know when it is appropriate to involve constituents, in this case parents, in decisions? A simple rule to remember is that the two prerequisites to a person's involvement in a decision are that (a) they must have a stake in the outcome, and (b) they must have the expertise to be involved. When one or both of these prerequisites is absent, then the leader must rethink whether or not involvement of others is appropriate.

If we apply these rules to the development or revision of a school's mission it becomes difficult to accept the failure to involve parents in this important act. Obviously, they have a stake in the outcome. All parents want their children to attend a school that has a strong and positive belief system. In fact, we are increasingly discovering that parents have some definite opinions about what some elements of the belief system ought to be. The first rule clearly exists.

This brings up the question of expertise. Do parents possess the expertise necessary to play a role in the development, articulation, and revision of a school's mission statement? I think that the answer to this question, in most cases, is certainly "Yes." There is no formal schooling required to develop a mission statement, as is the case with the charges of some other educational committees. The basic requirement in developing an organizational mission statement is that an individual is a part of that organization. As a part of the organization, an individual possesses the expertise to contribute to an understanding of what the organization ought to stand for. As Stephen Covey says, "Many organizations have a mission statement, but typically, people aren't committed to it because they aren't involved in developing it; consequently it's not part of the culture" (1990, p. 165). If we want parents to be committed to our school mission statements, then we must include them in the developing and continual revisions of it.

PARENTS—
VISITORS OR CRIMINALS?

In the past few years, I have been fortunate to visit many schools in different regions of the country. Regardless of where I am, one of the common elements in most of these schools is that they have some sort of visitor sign-in policy. That is, it is quite uncommon to visit an American school nowadays without being required to sign-in, and in many cases receive a badge, at the main office before proceeding to any other part of the school. I do not need to assist you in recalling many of the horrors of recent years that are responsible for precipitating these policies. These events and other societal changes that we have all witnessed have required schools to be increasingly concerned with who is inside the building while students are in attendance. Gone are the days when parents can enter school buildings unannounced without first being accounted for in the main office.

While these policies have become commonplace in our schools, the means by which they are announced and enforced differ from one another dramatically. In some schools, there are signs on the doors using language similar to the following:

> **"Stop! All visitors must sign-in at the office before proceeding further."**

Many of these announcements are on posters shaped and colored to resemble stop signs. While I applaud these schools for putting the safety of students first, does the message need to be delivered in this fashion? Consider the following example:

> **"Welcome to our school! We are so glad that you are here! We do ask that all visitors please sign-in at the office upon entering."**

Which message has a friendlier tone? Which message is more likely to make you really feel welcome? Most importantly, which message is most consistent with the language of your school's current mission statement?

In almost every case, the answers to these three questions all point to the second message. Some may argue that the forceful language in the first example is necessary. Without such forcefulness, people would not listen. I maintain that individuals who would ignore a message that says "Welcome to our school! We are so glad that you are here. We do ask that all visitors please sign-in at the office upon entering" are also more likely to ignore a more forceful message. In the meantime, by utilizing a forceful message, we have unintentionally made some of our more positive visitors feel unwelcome in our school because of the rather unfriendly edict that greeted them.

The odds are that the same people will report to the office no matter how the message is delivered. The negative effect that the message has on otherwise positive people is what concerns me. Most schools have mission statements that utilize such terms as "family," "caring adults," or "positive environment." A greeting that says, "Stop! All visitors must sign-in at the office before proceeding further" does not support any of those terms. Considering that it is also not likely to cause any more people to report to the office upon entering the school, such statements are counterproductive and severely hurt parental involvement and the creation of a positive school culture. Too often, in our busy and hectic schedules, we focus too heavily on the message while ignoring the method of delivery. Both are significant.

A related concern involves the use of "badges" that visitors wear when they are in school buildings. In a nutshell, the purpose of these badges is to identify the visitor and/or show individuals who are in regular attendance (i.e., students and staff) that this visitor has, in fact, already reported to the office. I have been in schools where only some of the visitors were wearing these badges. For the most part, these visitors fell into one of two categories. Either they were (a) individuals who rarely visited the school and would not be recognized by many people, or (b) highly recognized people who habitually follow rules. Other visitors, typically those who were often in the school and were known by virtually everybody, wandered around without having first picked up a badge in the office. In many cases, rather than risk insulting these people by confronting them, staff members in these schools allowed the visitors to be in the school without badges. This is unfair and upsetting to many parents. Consider the message we are giving visitors when we only require some of them to wear visitors badges. Though not necessarily intentional, we are saying that highly recognized visitors hold status different from those who only visit us occasionally. Either everybody should wear a visitors badge or nobody should. Today, with the safety concerns our schools have, the best answer is for everybody to wear them.

UTILIZING PARENTS TO IMPROVE SCHOOL CULTURE

As we know, students achieve more when their parents are involved in their education. Additionally, we know that parents are more likely to be involved if they truly believe that they are welcome in the school. The question many school leaders have is, "How can I involve parents in a way that will improve the culture of my school?"

For starters, we must go back to the mission statement. Parents ought to be involved, as I have said, in the creation and subsequent examinations and modifications of these statements. Doing so not only ensures that parents understand what the school is really all about, but it also allows parents to be involved at a foundational level. It is far more gratifying to be involved in discussions regarding a school's purpose than it is to only have involvement sought on mechanical issues such as how to more quickly and efficiently move the lunch lines.

That being said, it is also vitally important to involve parents in such issues as the efficient movement of the lunch lines. These issues involving day-to-day school operations, as all school leaders know, are important. They are just not the only way to utilize parental input.

PARENT ADVISORY COUNCILS

As I mentioned previously, the creation of a Parent Advisory Council is an excellent component of positive parental involvement. What is most important to understand, however, is the nature and purpose of creating such groups. That is to say, a Parent Advisory Council must not merely be an extension of an already existing parent group. Rather, it must be advisory in nature as its name suggests. The principal must utilize this group as an advising body on issues of real importance if the council is to be of any real value. If they are unwilling to do this, then it would be better to just not have a Parent Advisory Council at all. Committing to forming and utilizing a Parent Advisory Council requires that this group truly serve an advisory function. Otherwise, its existence can seem belittling to parents and will undoubtedly wind up harming the school culture it purports to help.

Below are examples of issues that Parent Advisory Councils can be charged with advising. As with all lists, they are merely suggestions. Obviously, in your school you will tailor the work of the Parent Advisory Council to meet your needs. Some guiding principles of successful councils are to:

- Encourage and assist parents to feel more comfortable in the school.
- Advance and develop parents' roles as educators in the home.
- Enhance communication between parents, community members, students, the school administration, the school staff, and the school board.
- Provide a formal means of consultation and recommendation for budgetary matters, curriculum issues, instructional programs, facilities, equipment, and learning resources.
- Ensure that there are relevant and effective procedures in place for students and their parents to communicate concerns.
- Initiate and maintain supportive activities for the school.

The list of guiding principles and activities of a Parent Advisory Council could go on almost endlessly. The important consideration, as previously mentioned, is that the function of such organizations must be on issues of significance for the school. When that is the case, then parents will realize that the school leadership values them as important components of a successful school. Parent input in these councils is about more than bake sales and other fundraisers. The improvements in school culture that come about when parents recognize their worth and value pays dividends that are hard to measure, but exist nevertheless.

Nothing here is intended to demean bake sales, fundraisers, or any other types of parent groups. To the contrary, these things are also vitally important to the success of a school. I, myself, have served as the vice-president of an elementary school PTA while my oldest daughter was in Kindergarten. This service took place in a school that had both a PTA and a Parent Advisory Council. The PTA, which met more frequently than did the Parent Advisory Council, was mostly involved in fundraising and preparations for special days. My creative excitement for elementary schools was a better match for that organization than it was for the proceedings of the Parent Advisory Council. The important thing was that this particular school had both of these organizations. When the only role of parents is to plan parties and fundraising activities, then schools are limiting the uses of these valuable resources.

PARENT RESOURCE ROOMS

During the tenure of my first school principalship, it became apparent that the parents in my community did not always feel welcome or comfortable in our school. This was unfortunate for so many different reasons. Chief among them was the fact that in this community many parents were available during the school day. The unemployment rate was higher than it was in some surrounding communities and the traditional values of the community were such that many mothers chose to stay at home during the day. Unlike the situation in many other schools, there was an abundance of resource help, in the form of parents, available to us whenever we wanted it. However, as I am sure you understand, availability is but one necessary component of getting parents involved in a school. What is true in the movies is not always true in education. If we build it, they do not necessarily come. Instead, parents need a reason to come to our schools. For many of them, particularly those of them who have suffered through some of their own negative school experiences, finding a reason is often easier said than done. Hence, the situation existed in which parents were available, but only a select few routinely involved themselves in the school. The task we faced, as builders and brokers of a positive school culture, was to give parents a reason to be involved.

Largely because of dictates from the Central Administrative Office, each school in this system had a site-based council, which was to assist in many of the major decisions previously reserved for the administration. The council at our school was comprised of three teachers, the school social worker, one parent representative, and myself. Since it was an obvious problem and because I am a firm believer in the valuable role parents play in their children's education, increasing parent involvement was the first charge our site-based council took on. After much discussion, analysis of parent survey data and school building needs, and discussions with the entire staff, we decided to open a Parent Resource Room in the school. Our goals for this room were simple. First, we wanted it to be a place where parents could come to get information that would be helpful to them, as parents. Second, we wanted the room to serve as a place where parents could do work and perform tasks that would be of benefit to students and teachers. Third, we wanted parents to feel some ownership in this room so that it would be a safe and welcoming place within the school in which they could gather.

The room was designed with all of these goals in mind. One wall of the Parent Resource Room was devoted to parenting materials (pamphlets, books, videos, and games) that the Social Worker provided. These were available for parents to check out, or they could be viewed and explored while the parent stayed in the room.

On this side of the room, there was a carpeted area with two rocking chairs for parents to sit in and, we hoped, feel a sense of comfort. On the opposite wall, we put up a large shelving unit. On this shelving unit, we placed a large bin for each teacher, labeled with their name. When teachers found themselves facing those tasks that were difficult for them to find time for but important to their classroom culture, they placed the materials and instructions for completing these tasks inside their bin. Projects placed in the bins ranged from simple bulletin board tasks such as cutting out letters, to the creation of art projects, to the development of mathematics flash cards, and beyond. At the base of this wall and extending into the center of the room were two long tables surrounded by chairs.

An important component of the Parent Resource Room was one long wall, which I encouraged parents to decorate as they saw fit. With this power, they decided to put painted handprints of students all over the wall. Not only was this appropriate decor for an elementary school, but the design of it empowered the parents and gave them a real sense of ownership in the room.

I would be guilty of a grandiose lie if I said that the creation of this room magically transformed parents' attitudes and lead them in flocks to be involved in our school. Over time, however, the results were very close to a flock of parents becoming involved. At first, the same few parents who were always involved, spent time in the room. As we advertised it in my weekly newsletter, a few more got involved. There was a sense of security for some parents in knowing that this room belonged to them. They still needed to visit the office upon entering the school building, but they were then free to go to *their* room. Many of them, to the delight of our staff, worked for teachers while in the room. Some of them, I know, simply sat in the room and visited, slowly but surely building up their level of comfort at being in the school at all.

As word spread of the parent Resource Room, one of our parent volunteers contacted the local newspaper. As a result, we had a full-page story touting the room's benefits. This, along with the praises being sung by the teachers who benefitted from the parents' efforts, made the room a very popular site in our school building. Not only were our three original goals accomplished, but there were many other benefits, as well.

- ◆ There was at least one small corner of the school in which all parents felt welcome.

- ◆ Students of this community, for the first time, got very used to parents being in the building. This helped create a bond between school and home.

- ◆ Teachers began to see parents as very helpful and much less threatening and critical than they had once perceived them to be.

- ◆ Parents knew what went on in the school building on a regular basis. While they were not roaming the halls, due to the distraction I felt that would cause for students' learning, they were in the

building. They could feel the climate on a regular
basis.

♦ Most significantly, for the first time in many of
their lives, the parents of this school were a valuable, integral part of the school's culture.

We were very fortunate to have a vacant room in this
school for the creation of a Parent Resource Room. This, I understand, is not a luxury all schools enjoy. I am confident that
had we not had a room, we would have worked at accomplishing these goals in another way. That is the challenge facing many of you. In the absence of space, can you make parents feel more welcome in your school? Can you provide resources that are helpful to parents, while expecting nothing in
return? Can you include parents in a way that makes them feel
as if the school is partly their school?

Again, as is the case with much of what I have said, we
first need to believe that there are great benefits in involving
parents in their children's education. We must understand
that the strongest, most positive school cultures are the ones in
which this involvement exists. Furthermore, we must understand the barriers to parental involvement that exist today. I,
like many readers, have struggled with difficult parents. I
have had my moments, as I know you have, in which I have
wished parents would just go away. It is true that parents of
today can present challenges for school leaders, which may
lead to frustration and, in the worst cases, disgust. Do yourself
and your students a favor, though. Work at building bridges
with parents that will improve our schools. Parents are valuable allies who can enhance a school in so many wonderful
ways. If we manage the frustrations and sincerely ask these allies to join us in our mission, then we will unquestionably
strengthen our schools and provide our students with positive
cultures.

SUMMARY OF KEY POINTS

♦ As more and more people begin to understand the
powerful role parents play in their children's education, all schools must look closely at the ways in

which they attempt to keep this vital constituent group welcomed and involved.

♦ School personnel need to understand the importance of parents and must work hard to understand parents' perspectives.

♦ To involve parents in a manner that would directly impact student achievement, it is necessary for school leaders to include them in the development, articulation, and continuous revision of the school's mission statement.

♦ Parents are more likely to be involved if they truly believe that they are welcome in the school.

♦ The improvements in school culture that come about when parents recognize their worth and value pays dividends that are hard to measure, but exist nevertheless.

6

HELPING OURSELVES BY FIRST HELPING OTHERS: THE STUDENT'S ROLE

If the education of our youth is really the fundamental reason for school's existence, as I insist it is, then the students are unquestionably the most important individuals in our schools. That being said, it is patently illogical for us to focus on creating, fostering, and sustaining positive school cultures without closely examining the role of the student. Students, we must always remember, are much more than mere receivers of the information dispensed by adults. They are, or we should at least strive to make them, active participants in education. In this regard, their roles in schooling and in the creation of school cultures are not passive ones. Rather, students are active creators of our school cultures and are willing participants in all of the experiences that the culture provides. As beneficiaries of these positive cultures, students must recognize the paramount significance of their role. They cannot do so without our assistance, though. For though we are not called to fill their empty cups, we educators surely must guide students. Therefore, helping students to help themselves ought to be our primary call as servant leaders.

We provide this help in a variety of ways. The most common and easiest way to understand it is in the creation of student organizations whose purposes, either stated or implied, are to create or enhance positive cultures. These student organizations exist at all levels, from elementary schools through high schools. Where student organizations were once entities reserved for high school in order to help prepare students for the working world, they are now found throughout K-12 education. Though they differ from one another in many of their goals and practices, they do share a few common elements. These elements, all of which contribute to the development of a positive school culture and are therefore vitally important, are described below.

♦ **They empower students**

Student organizations, from student councils to peer mediation programs empower students to lead and to take responsibility. This empowerment automatically raises the stake students have in school governance to a higher level. It gives them a sense of ownership, which is so vitally important. When students are empowered, they are more likely to "buy into" a school's mission.

♦ **They provide extra-curricular involvement**

Whether a student organization holds its meetings outside of the regular school day (as many of them do) or not, students have some degree of involvement in the organization apart from what they do during their regular school hours. This involvement may take the form of something as simple as planning activities outside of the school day.

♦ **They involve service to the school**

Student organizations serve the school community in a variety of ways. Whether they are peer mediation programs that help reduce violence or student councils that sponsor a multitude of events, student organizations keep students involved in a "service mentality."

♦ **They teach responsibility**

Inherent in participation in most student organizations is the need for students to be responsible. One of the benefits of being involved in student organizations is that students learn to manage their time more effectively and, thus become increasingly responsible. Additionally, they learn the importance of working with others in a group environment.

Now, consider for a moment the importance of these four elements, particularly as they relate to the creation and sustenance of positive school cultures. Why, for example, is it important for us to empower students? How will doing so contribute to the development of a positive school culture? For one thing, when students are empowered they are receiving a message that the adults in the school believe they are capable. When a Student Council is given latitude to direct its efforts in a school community, the empowered members are indirectly being told that they are able to accomplish things for the betterment of the school community without adult intervention. This is vitally important in the development of students' self-concepts. Of equal importance is the sense of ownership such empowerment helps students to feel regarding their school. The school community begins to feel more like it belongs partially to them and less like something owned by already educated adults.

In the case of Peer Mediation or Conflict Resolution programs, students are empowered to solve their own problems and resolve their own conflicts. Again, the sense of ownership this gives students allows them to feel more involved and potentially more important to the creation of a safe and orderly school environment. Contrast the message students receive from these programs with what they are traditionally told. Namely, that adult intervention is needed in order for students to resolve a disagreement. A message such as this does little to prepare students for life and even less for developing the feelings of self-worth and belonging characteristic of a positive culture. Empowerment leads to responsibility, which in turn, leads to feelings of self worth. In fact, as motivational theories have shown us (Herzberg, 1993), people are motivated when they feel responsible, recognized, and appreciated. Students in schools with positive cultures are often far more motivated than are their counterparts in schools with negative cultures. This is largely due to the recognition and appreciation they feel from adult members of the school community. Empowerment is the catalyst for much of this recognition and these subsequent feelings of self-worth.

Student organizations help students to connect the idea of school with activities that they enjoy and find rewarding. Though many high achieving students participate in extracurricular activities, there are also many students who struggle with school benefitting from such involvement. For these students, who otherwise might not enjoy school as much as their higher achieving counterparts because of their academic struggles, extra-curricular offerings are a great way to associate school with a place where they can engage in something that they find positive and rewarding. This has an obviously positive impact on the school's culture. The more students who can find something at school that engages them in a positive way, the better they will feel about being at school. In addition, the higher achieving students also benefit from extra-curricular involvement. Though they may find academics more rewarding than lower achieving classmates do, extra-curricular involvements present new and unique challenges for them as well.

A positive school culture, as we all know, is one in which stakeholders believe in and care about the school. Extra-curricular activities, from those already mentioned to sports activities to the performing arts, all provide opportunities for students to serve the school community. Whether the service takes the form of making school more peaceful or merely providing entertainment, students engaging in extra-curricular activities are certainly serving their schools. This not only helps to teach students about the importance of servant leadership, a concept that will serve them later in life, but it helps to create a positive school culture because it leads students to a greater sense of caring about the school.

Finally, the sense of responsibility that students gain from participating in student organizations improves their ability to succeed in all venues. Since responsibility is a necessary component of service organizations, athletic teams, and almost all other extra-curricular and co-curricular programs, students can transfer the responsibility learned through participation in these activities to all other aspects of their schooling. Lastly, because responsibility for schoolwork is a co-requisite of participating in many of these programs, students have a greater need to remain responsible about their academic achievement. Aside from the personal benefits gained for students, this, too, positively impacts the culture of the school. It does so because it forces students to stay focused on academic achievement.

The imperative for school leaders, therefore, is to provide organizations for students, which will contribute to and reflect the mission statement of the school. If a school's mission contains any of the more popular, widely used elements such as "creating lifelong learners," "helping students reach their potential," or "fostering responsibility," then involvement in student organizations may provide necessary assistance toward reaching this goal. Such organizations should involve as many of the three previously described elements as possible in order to provide maximum benefit.

Recognizing students who participate in these organizations is often as important as recognizing those who exhibit great academic achievement. If this is not the case in your particular school, then I urge you to reexamine your mission. As has been previously mentioned, schools exist in order to educate our youth. In this regard, academics are naturally of real importance. However, part of educating a child, or any person for that matter, is to draw out from that person the skills and talents which they already possess. The skilled educator must then develop or enhance those innate skills. As we all know, for some children these skills and talents lie in physical activity, music, theater, or interpersonal relations. For the students possessing these talents, their development is an important part of their own, particular education. As students enhance these skills, then recognition for their efforts is vitally important. Remember, students who are recognized are often motivated. Those who are motivated to do well will positively enhance the culture of our schools.

IMPROVING STUDENT ACHIEVEMENT

As we have repeatedly mentioned, the most significant roles of our schools are to first create an environment in which students achieve and then to ensure that such achievement actually takes place. We necessarily define the desired achievement differently from one community to the next. A benchmark score on a standardized test cannot always pinpoint the achievement desired. If it could, then there would be an underlying assumption that all of our schools contained student populations that were intellectually equal. The Normal Curve would cease to be an assumption of the entire population it measured performance against and would instead become a curve that is representative of all individual school populations. Such an assumption, all educators know, is patently absurd. Many of you have worked in more than one school. Some of you have worked in environments with populations drastically different from one another. Was the intellectual capacity of student populations in each of these schools identical to the intellectual capacity of those in other schools? Of course not.

Consider this additional fact about the Normal Curve. The mean, or midpoint, on the Normal Curve of standard IQ tests is a score of 115. Such tests have a standard deviation of 10. Does that mean that in any school, anywhere in the United States, the measurement of all students' IQs would yield a mean of 115? Well, I have worked in a school where the mean for the entire student population was surely one standard deviation above, thereby creating a schoolwide mean of 125. Similarly, my first principalship occurred in a school where the mean was at least one standard deviation below, creating a schoolwide mean of 105 or less. Many readers have similar, or even more profound, experiences. What this tells us is that all schools cannot measure gains in student achievement in the same manner. There cannot be one benchmark that all of us must measure student performance against. Sound school leadership is required for each school community to determine its own benchmarks. This leadership must occur at the local level with people who understand the populations they serve. The more stakeholders that are involved in this understanding, the better the school community is able to judge student success.

Not only do schools with positive cultures involve all stakeholders in the creation of their missions, but they also ensure that all stakeholders understand what constitutes student success in their community. With this information in hand, there can be realistic, schoolwide efforts to improve student achievement. School constituents, from parents to teachers to students can assist in the efforts with a common understanding of what constitutes success. This common understanding is what is missing in so many of our schools. Despite what the media and the politicians sometimes want us to believe, it is not about how many Merit Scholars our schools have. It is about how well our students are reaching their honest potential.

The question this brings up regards whether or not any of the co-curricular or extra-curricular programs previously discussed really lend themselves to improved academic performance of students. If they do not, then despite the benefits they create for our school cultures, are they really worthwhile? Some would argue that the answer is, "No." The good news, which renders any debate over this issue useless, is that evidence suggests that such involvements do, in fact, contribute in many cases to increases in student performance. Chalkley (1989), in a study whose results have been replicated with different student populations, discovered that participating in extra-curricular activities while in high school did not lead to a sacrifice of academics. In fact, she reported, participating in such activities can often boost grades. This large-scale study was completed over a six-year period and involved over 14,000 students.

There is additionally other significant support in the literature for the notion that participation in after school student organizations, in general, contributes to stronger academic performance, decreases the dropout rate, and strengthens students' interpersonal skills (Braddock, Dawkins, & Wilson, 1995). Enhanced student learning is even more profound in the case of extra-curricular activities that are aligned with school curricula, such as language clubs and social studies groups.

As is the case with any educational programs, the proposed benefits must be examined in light of what is already known about the school population. Co-curricular and extra-curricular activities have been correlated with increased student achievement in many schools. In addition, participation in these programs has many benefits for school culture. Most notably, as I have illustrated, student programs and organizations empower students, give them an increased sense of responsibility, and involve them more in school operations. All of these elements can contribute to the creation and sustenance of a positive school culture. The key, which must be remembered, is an already existing culture in which stakeholders are involved. When more people understand the population characteristics and mission of a school, then they are better equipped to create opportunities for students that will lead to academic achievement and cultural improvements.

INVOLVING STUDENTS
IN OTHER WAYS

While student organizations can be one significant way of utilizing students in the creation of a positive school culture, a lack of formal student organizations ought not to be cause for despair. Many schools across the nation keep students involved in their culture through much less formal means. In these schools, there are daily opportunities for students to contribute to the school culture and to be recognized for doing so.

For example, literally thousands of schools engage themselves in some form of "Caught Being Good" activities. For those of you who may be unfamiliar with this concept, activities like these involve nothing more than a commitment from staff members to report to the office the names of all students "caught" doing something especially good during the school day. These students are then publicly recognized for their deeds. This recognition can, and generally, does take a variety of forms. Whether the recognition comes in the form of a certificate from the principal or the students' names being announced over the intercom is irrelevant. What is relevant is that the students receive some form of recognition for engaging in behavior that is supportive of a positive school culture. This, in turn, reinforces and reminds all students of the types of behaviors valued as positive by their school community.

When an activity such as this is an integral part of the school's culture, it requires very little time and very few resources. As such, it is not difficult for any school to engage in. This simplicity makes it an attractive part of many positive school cultures. Now, consider the benefits of this concept in light of the elements described earlier in this chapter, as associated with the benefits of formal student organizations. Do they apply to these less formal endeavors?

Consider the first one. If students are recognized for doing something good, be it assisting a less able student with a task or putting forth their best effort on an assignment, they are being empowered to behave honorably and appropriately. The mere recognition of a student who does something good empowers that student to continue doing good because it reinforces the values of the school community. Consider this analogy: If readers of this book inform me that it was beneficial to them and their school community, then I receive a swift reminder of what they value. I, as a result, become empowered to write other books that may be beneficial to them.

The reverse, as is usually the case, is also true here. When students are only "caught" doing bad things, then they are disempowered. While they are reminded of the behaviors that are not valued by the school community, they are not empowered to behave appropriately because they may not know which behaviors are deemed appropriate. This sense of disempowerment can be damaging to a school's culture. Obviously, we must correct inappropriate behavior. However, if we do so while also recognizing behavior that is deemed appropriate and positive, then we are empowering students to make appropriate choices.

Catching students doing something good also allows students to provide service to the school. Consider what happens when a group of students engage in a school beautification project. This does not need to be in the form of a student organization, say a Student Council, cleaning up the school grounds. Instead, this can merely be a group of students who take it upon themselves to pick up some trash on the school grounds. When they are "caught" doing this and are consequently recognized for their positive actions, then two important things take place. The students are providing service to the school, and they are being recognized for their positive efforts. Indeed, they will learn to be more responsible, and they will be empowered to continue behaving in a positive manner. Both of these outcomes are associated with positive school cultures.

Finally, we must consider the benefits catching students doing something good has for the rest of the student population. These students hear the public praise bestowed on their classmates, even if they themselves are not the recipients of it. This reinforces the values of the school community. As a result, there is a better chance that all students will behave appropriately because appropriate behavior is being redefined on a regular basis for them. All students see examples of what constitutes "good." Consider how different this is from being in an environment where children are only acknowledged for behaving badly. Again, in those environments the efforts are on defining what "not to do". Students need to be shown what "to do" instead. Then, when they do it, they deserve to be recognized. In the world of academics, we do not showcase all of the students who earn D's and F's, do we? We do not invite the school community to an assembly of the "Dishonor Roll," right? No, we do not. The reason for this is quite simple. We choose to honor those who achieve academically partly to keep them motivated and valued and partly to present a positive model to the rest of the student body. The same logic ought to be employed as we recognize students for achievements in realms that are not purely academic.

One last point worth mentioning here involves the idea of how to make praise work most effectively. Ben Bissell (1992) lists five important elements that make praise work most effectively:

♦ Effective praise must be **authentic**.

This means that the praise must be based on something that is really true. When people perceive that they are being praised for something that is not true or authentic, the praise can take on a very patronizing meaning.

- Effective praise must be **specific**.

  By being specific in our praise, we increase the likelihood that the positive behavior will be repeated. If, for example, a child is told that he or she is "good," they are often left wondering what it is that makes them "good." Being praised for a specific action (i.e., helping another student solve a mathematics problem) informs everybody of the specific behavior that you approved of.

- Effective praise is **immediate**.

  If too much time passes between the positive action and the praise, then there is an increased chance that the recipient will forget having done something praiseworthy. While assemblies that recognize student achievement are obviously not immediate, they are effective as long as students have been receiving immediate praise in the interim.

- Effective praise must be **clean**.

  This means that it comes with "no strings attached." Clean praise contains no qualifiers. It is not intended to manipulate the recipient into doing something else. Clean praise is honest praise, which expects nothing in return.

- Effective praise is given in **private**.

  Because people are sometimes embarrassed by public praise, praise that is privately given is the most effective. However, if all praise is given in private, then we miss the opportunity for others to benefit by positive examples. Therefore, I recommend a combination of public and private praise with students. Give them the more effective private praise, but also praise publicly so that others understand what the desired behaviors are. The public praise will most readily improve the overall culture.

STUDENTS: INTEGRAL
PARTS OF SCHOOL CULTURE

When I was a teacher in northwest Indiana, I was involved in both structured student organizations and less formal student recognition programs, similar to "Caught Being Good." Both of these endeavors contributed positively to the school's positive culture. I describe them here as examples of what can be a synergistic relationship between both formally structured student organizations and far less formal activities designed to empower students to positively impact a school's culture.

In the late 1980s and the early 1990s, there was a steady infusion of conflict resolution programs across the public schools in our country. The well-publicized examples of school violence in recent years, has created an even larger explosion of these programs into the curriculum of almost all school communities. I helped to found the program at my school, and I witnessed firsthand the cultural benefits conflict resolution brought to this school. To put this into context and to get us all on the proverbial "same page," I offer the following summation of the program I was fortunate to be involved in.

The Conflict Management Program at this elementary school believed:

♦ Happiness is not the absence of conflict, but the ability to cope with it.

♦ Conflict is a natural, often beneficial part of relationships.

♦ We can grow through conflict.

♦ Students are capable of solving their own conflicts.

♦ Students should be empowered, whenever appropriate, to solve their own conflicts.

♦ Students should be empowered, whenever appropriate, to assist other students as mediators of their conflicts.

◆ Teachers should teach Conflict Resolution skills to all students.

◆ Parents should support the Conflict Resolution skills taught in our curriculum.

These beliefs, well synchronized with the school's mission statement, set the foundation for a formal program that transformed the culture of this school. Keep in mind, however, that beliefs alone cannot do this. It worked at our school because the above mentioned beliefs became the collective beliefs of stakeholders. As discussed earlier, when beliefs are developed collectively, that is when they represent the beliefs of administrators, teachers, staff members, parents, and students, then they have the power to result in transformations. It is also necessary to note that this school employed a social worker, Elizabeth Douglas, who embodied all of the traits of a positive leader. As such, her leadership and guidance were keys to making this and so many other programs successful. She, better than anybody I have ever met, understood the importance of involving stakeholders in the creation of a positive school culture. As this book goes to press, Liz continues to improve the culture of that school.

While this Conflict Management Program was growing, this particular school continued to engage itself in many of the less formal activities that involved students so well in the creation and sustenance of the school's positive culture. One of these activities, the brainchild of Principal Douglas Hollar, was the school's Citizen of the Week program. In this endeavor, each week one teacher at each grade level was asked to identify a student that exemplified good citizenship. This did not need to be a student who achieved great things academically, but instead, needed to be a student who behaved responsibly and honorably toward colleagues. This student was congratulated by the principal, photographed, and given a certificate, which was displayed in the hallway for all to see that week.

This student-centered school also had a program during this time period called B.U.G., which was an acronym for Bringing Up Grades. This involved rewarding students at the end of each grading period, in a public ceremony, for improving their grades over the last grading period. The student did not need to be a straight A student. Instead, it was required that the student merely improve their grades from the last time they had been reported. These students received an award and also had their names displayed for all to see. The school also had an Honor Roll system, which recognized students for consistently high achievement. These students may have been unable to improve their grades because they consistently achieved high results. Honor Roll, as it is in many schools, was designed to recognize them.

These engagements, both formal and informal, do not represent everything that went on at this school of a co-curricular or extra-curricular nature. There was a student council, an intramural sports program, and a choir among the several other activities for students to be a part of. The point here is not ·o mention and discuss all of these activities, but to describe the synergistic relationship and subsequent positive impact on the school's culture that they all had. It is also significant to note that there were opportunities for all students to be involved and recognized for some positive contribution they had made. While the school's efforts were certainly centered heavily on academic achievement, educating the "whole child" necessitated that opportunities existed for recognition of all forms of positive achievement.

At this northwest Indiana school, students were recognized for achievements, improvements, and positive character traits on a regular basis. Some students participated in structured programs, which led to this recognition, while others merely experienced their benefits as part of their ordinary school days. They were inescapable parts of the school's culture, though. The formal, structured programs, suːh as Conflict Management and Student Council supported the beliefs and mission of the school that were exhibited through the less formal activities such as Citizen of the Week. The less formal activities supported the beliefs of the more formal, structured programs, as well. The result of these synergistic, intertwined relationships was a positive school culture that had student empowerment, service, and responsibility at its essence.

INVOLVING STUDENTS
IN ALL SCHOOLS

Similar, exciting, student-centered activities take place at schools all across America on a regular basis. Though affective in nature, they also contribute greatly, as I have tried to illustrate, to an increase in student achievement. As such, they have a tremendous, positive impact on the culture of our schools. These activities and these student organizations need not only take the forms of those described in this chapter, however. What our schools need, more than programs that fit my short descriptions, are leaders who recognize the benefits of such programs. These leaders, who must really understand their own school community, can then adapt what I have described to fit their own schools. Some of you, for example, may find great difficulty in organizing programs after regular school hours. This could be so for a variety of reasons, from students needing to work after school to strong teacher associations that prohibit such practices. Others of you cannot schedule co-curricular activities that take place during the school day due to space and/or scheduling restrictions. It is up to you, therefore, to adapt. Believe in the value of incorporating students into the development of a positive school cultures, first. Once that belief is a part of you, then you will discover options unknown to me that will surely work for your school community.

We need to remember that students must be involved in creating, fostering, and sustaining positive school cultures. To leave them out is to ignore the very souls of our schools. In this adult world in which we live, it is easy to forget the children as we rush to use our expertise to create schools for them. Children have the ability and all of the necessary skills and tools to have positive impacts on our schools' cultures, and to consequently rid our schools of many of their contemporary ills. We must believe this first. Once we truly believe it, we will be well on the way to helping them to create these student-empowered opportunities. Then, as this chapter's title insinuates, we must allow students to help others by first helping themselves.

SUMMARY OF KEY POINTS

♦ It is patently illogical for us to focus on creating, fostering, and sustaining positive school cultures without closely examining the role of the student.

♦ Student organizations empower students, provide extra-curricular involvement, involve service to the school, and teach responsibility.

♦ Students in schools with positive cultures are often far more motivated than are their counterparts in schools with negative cultures.

♦ Students should receive some form of recognition for engaging in behavior that is supportive of a positive school culture.

♦ Children have the ability and all of the necessary skills and tools to have positive impacts on our schools' cultures, and to consequently rid our schools of many of their contemporary ills.

7

GETTING TO THE HEART: BUILDING COMMUNITY SCHOOLS

Schools cannot be seen as places of fragmentation. The principal cannot have one job to do, while the teachers and staff have others. Parents cannot fill one niche, performing in isolation from all others, and students cannot operate apart from adults, in isolation. If they could, then schools would be like factories with job specialization as the rule. The outputs of all school-based efforts would be nearly identical, and the heart and soul of schools would grow silent. None of the elements of positive school cultures could be present. There would be no concern for confluence of values, and though there may be a common mission on paper, it would be arrived at through separate, disconnected tasks. The many benefits of positive, family-like cultures would give way to the dangers and damages of negative, detached cultures.

Instead, schools must operate as communities. In this way, it is expected that people would perform different roles and have different responsibilities, but a common mission that stakeholders truly embraced would exist. Principals, teachers, staff, parents, and students would engage in different tasks, but they would do so to arrive at the same place, namely a positive school in which the culture celebrates their diversity and rewards their achievements. The sense of community that our schools must have implicitly implies that all stakeholders must work together in order that they may achieve together.

The idea that schools should operate as communities is not new in education. Nor is it an idea that has not been alluded to over and over again throughout this book. In fact, researchers have understood this need for years, and I have given examples of what schools as communities are like in each chapter of this book. Think back to our analogy of the giant patchwork quilt. A quilt is analogous to a community in many ways. The different

111

patches on the quilt are representative of the different members of a community. Each one is distinct and has its own qualities, but each one also plays an interdependent role in the creation of the whole. The thread that binds the quilt together, representative here of the school culture, plays the same role in a community. It holds everybody together as it touches everybody and binds individuals to one another.

When schools operate as communities, then they accomplish great things, just as in the example of the community playground from Chapter 2. That building project, which truly was a labor of love for those who engaged in it, involved people from all walks of life. There were those present whom we would expect to be present, contractors, carpenters, politicians, and media personnel. However, there were also people like me working on the project. As somebody who needs to stare at a screwdriver for several minutes as I contemplate which way I should turn it to get the desired effect, I am not one who is traditionally seen building things. Because of the strong sense of community that existed during this project, I could not imagine myself being anyplace else, though. In short, I was not drawn to the community playground-building project because of an interest in or aptitude for building. I was drawn to it for the sense of community, which made me feel like I belonged.

Such a strong sense of community participation is precisely what our schools need. We should certainly see the people whom we would expect to see involved in a school, just as we should certainly see carpenters building the playground. However, the best schools also find ways to include those individuals who are not traditionally found collaborating with a school. In the strongest school communities, even unlikely community members have an essential role to play. More significantly, they understand that role and its interdependence with other members of the school community.

Finally, consider the behaviors of the top-notch principals who were described in Chapter 3. These individuals understood the value of community involvement in their school's success. In my discussions with them, the words *family, positive, homey, comfortable, active, alive, servant, parents, diverse, open,* and *non-judgmental* were used as descriptors of the school culture. These words conjure up strong images of community for me. Are they not words that you would like people to use in describing your school? If these words were to be compared with the language used to describe negative school cultures, their differences would be as great as the difference between night and day.

This all leads up to the important question of "How"? How can the principal create a sense of community in their school? How can our schools become places in which community members want to be involved? How can we create the caring, open communities our students and their families deserve?

THE COMMUNITY PRINCIPAL

Thomas Sergiovanni (1995) reminds us that there is a difference between formal organizations and communities. Though they may have similar goals as communities, formal organizations form connections between and among people because of external controls, such as contracts. Communities, on the other hand, base their connections between people on commitments and values, ideas that are more internal. Schools, he argues, ought to more appropriately function as communities. When this happens, then schools can finally be defined as much more than brick and mortar. Relationships, values, and a sense of mission become better terms for defining schools.

This will necessarily change the role of the principal. As Sergiovanni says, "It is argued that as community takes hold in schools, the principal emerges as a true leader" (p. 78). Whereas formal organizations are usually managed, schools, as communities must be led. This, as your own experiences may prove, is one of the great ironies of being a school leader today. The age-old debate of management versus leadership boils down to much more than personal beliefs. The very institutional structure of our schools is a factor that cannot be ignored. As experience demonstrates, the formal organizational structures of some of our schools can be very constraining. Consider this example from one principal:

> I go almost every year to conventions for principals, and there's always a speech telling us we need to be educational leaders, not managers. It's a great idea. And yet, the system doesn't allow you to be an educational leader. Everyone wants the power to run the schools in one way or another-the central office, the union, the board, the parents, the special-interest groups. What's left for the principal to dictate isn't always very much. There's so little we have to control or to change. The power, the authority, is somewhere else, though not necessarily the responsibility. (Boyer, 1983, p 219)

This statement reflects the frustration a great many educational leaders often feel. Most of them want to be true leaders. It is this aspect of their jobs that is found to be most rewarding. Sadly though, many of our school leaders believe that their ability to lead has been taken away while their responsibility has increased. The challenges this creates, they feel, are very difficult to overcome. However, as examples from Chapter 3 have indicated, principals can and do rise above these challenges. It is not always easy, and it cannot be done alone. This is why the sense of community our schools need is so vitally important. When community feelings exist, then the sharing of responsibility becomes easier. When the sharing of responsibility is easier, then management tasks become more manageable. Finally, when management tasks are more manageable, then leaders are freer to lead.

This is another great irony. The very obstacles to becoming a leader are eliminated when schools operate as communities. While the transformation suggested here might be difficult at first, especially within a school system that operates as a formal organization, it becomes much easier over time. There are potentially some management tasks that must take on secondary importance at first, but once the school really begins to operate as a community, then those management tasks can be accomplished without constraining the leader's ability to lead.

Consider this analogy: I really want to begin a regular exercise regimen. Though I am not in terrible physical shape, there are tremendous health benefits to be gained by a regular exercise program. I understand that, and I am sincere when I say that I want to do it. However, it is very difficult, at first. I have the hardest time getting myself started. There seems to be too many other things to do, and I simply cannot regularly find the time to exercise. Have you heard arguments like this before?

What is likely to happen once I force myself to begin my exercise regimen? I am not talking about the first few days, but am instead thinking of a time period several weeks into the regimen. Research shows that once I get over that initial hump and the exercise regimen becomes an integral part of what I accomplish in a week, I will gain more energy and find myself able to accomplish everything I used to accomplish without giving up the exercise. The healthier I get, the more I can accomplish. The same is true for school leaders wishing to break out of the management paradigm they feel locked into. As they focus more on leading and creating a strong sense of community in their schools, they will find the management tasks that used to consume all of their time much easier to manage. They will become community principals. In this capacity, with the shared sense of mission inherent in strong communities, they will lead. Simply stated, to be a community leader, you must lead your community.

Make no mistake about it. Obstacles to creating a real sense of community exist for many of our schools. The process, for many, is not at all easy. Schools, wherever they exist on the community continuum, are dynamic organizations. As such, conflicting goals, beliefs, and attitudes can hamper any efforts. For this reason, this chapter cannot be taken out of context. Instead, it must be considered within the context of the rest of this book's message. Principals need to internalize the behaviors from Chapter 3 that are strongly associated with creating positive school cultures. Similarly, teachers must understand their tremendous power in creating strong classroom cultures. They must recognize their role in creating a strong sense of community in their own rooms on a regular basis. We all need to be further cognizant of the role parents play in our sense of schools as communities. We must involve them appropriately, so that our school cultures will be strengthened. In doing so, we will naturally increase the feelings of community present in our schools. The students cannot be ignored, either. We know that they are the very reason our schools exist and that their mark on our school cultures is lasting. Now, we also cannot forget the larger community in which our schools operate. They, too, play an invaluable role in strengthening our school cultures. Organizations and members of our community need to recognize what they offer to our schools and what our schools offer to them before they will become involved. It is up to us all to help the community in this regard.

BUSINESS PARTNERSHIPS

One of the more recent focuses of school-community relationships has been in the area of business partnerships. These partnerships, created for mutual benefit, have become an important component of a great many school-community relations plans. For those of you who may be unfamiliar with them, school-business partnerships have these characteristics:

♦ They involve two-way communication between school officials and business executives.

♦ Members of the business community assist the school in educating its students. They do this in a variety of ways. Examples include the donation of money or supplies and the providing of speakers for special occasions.

♦ Members of the school assist the business in accomplishing its goals. Examples of this assistance include having teachers or support staff visit the business to better understand its mission and having groups of students do volunteer work that is of assistance to the business.

♦ School-business partnerships are rarely one-time involvements. Instead, successful partnerships are ongoing.

Not only do these partnerships accomplish the goals of mutual assistance for each organization, but they also allow for the involvement of members of the business community in the missions of our educational institutions. In this way, they provide tremendous assistance to school leaders desiring a strong sense of community in their schools. The benefits of these business involvements are far reaching. Having allies in the business community can provide a great counter balance to any negative publicity our schools may undeservedly receive. When local business leaders, who tend to often be the same people who lead local civic organizations, have a positive opinion of your school, then it becomes less popular for people to say negative things about the school in the community.

A key point to consider is that these business partnerships do not happen automatically. While a reactive stance in a very commercial or industrial community may still yield business support, most school leaders need to be proactive in order to garner the kind of business support that is necessary. This is due to the fact that many of our schools exist in areas that are not heavily populated by businesses. An additional factor existing in communities that do have several businesses to partner with is that schools are often forced to compete for the same business partnerships. Principals and central office administrators who communicate with the larger community on a regular basis can best accomplish this. For this reason, I advocate two key points. First, school leaders ought to think seriously about ways in which they can communicate the goals and accomplishments of their schools to community members outside of the normal school community. It is not enough to send regular written communication home to parents, though it is a necessary thing to do. Instead, school leaders must also consider the benefits of sending these communications to members of the community whom do not have children in their school. High on this list ought to be leaders of local businesses who may otherwise have no way of knowing what really goes on in the local schools. If this is deemed too costly, then administrators ought to consider radio or other media communications such as a local access cable channel. Getting the messages out to the larger public is the school leader's responsibility.

Second, school leaders ought to involve themselves in local civic organizations and/or community boards. These types of community involvements are great ways for the smart administrator to meet and get to know leaders in the community. It is amazing how much informal communication can happen through these involvements, which can lead to great things for your school. Many a school business partnership has begun because of a friendship between the principal and the business leader that precipitated it.

In addition to business partnerships, it is worth noting that some of the same benefits can be derived from strong relationships with nonprofit organizations. Groups such as the Boy Scouts, Girl Scouts, local Little League and other youth sporting organizations, and the United Way are all interested in partnerships with schools. In return for the use of space and permission to distribute some of their materials, these organizations can offer schools great support in accomplishing some of their goals. In many schools, for example, these organizations donate items such as flags for the school to display. Additionally, they give schools plaques to display their allegiance and/or individual recognition pins that can be worn by staff members.

COMMUNITY SCHOOLS

At the heart of the concept of Community Schools lies the need across our country for Community Education. This is the understanding that all people in any given community can benefit from offerings within our schools. In essence it is a simple idea: schools are not merely institutions that teach children, but can and ought to be learning centers for the entire community because learning is a lifelong process.

Furthermore, Community Schools make use of the school facility far beyond the hours required of a traditional school day. For this reason, many people tout Community Schools as using community resources wisely. The extended hours allow for academic, cultural, recreational, civic, health, and social services for people in the community of all ages. Many people acknowledge this usefulness because, in reality, most schools in our nation are only used for a maximum of one third of their potential. Typically, a school is used less than eight hours a day, five days a week, nine months a year. Because facility maintenance and debt service costs continue year-round, as do people's educational, recreational, and social needs, many argue that we ought to maximize school facility usage. Another factor that makes schools so appealing for community usage is their location. Most schools are located in a place that makes them the center of a community. As such, people find them easily accessible.

The programs offered in a Community School may be very different from one community to the next. These programs and their availability have a great deal to do with the needs and resources of the local community. In an examination of Community Schools, the following are among the most common components:

- Pre-school and after-school child care programs;
- Remedial and enrichment activities for school children;
- Family support and family education programs;
- Health and human service programs;
- Recreation activities for adults and children;
- Programs for senior citizens;
- Literacy programs;
- English as a second language programs;
- Civic and citizenship programs;
- Workforce preparation programs; and
- Career and technical skills upgrading programs.

These, and the countless other specific components of Community Schools have so many benefits for the communities of our nation. Many of them can be accomplished at a cost far below what it would be if the various organizations needed to find their own facilities for offering these services. As such, they represent moral leadership in a very strong way. School leaders who allow the community into their schools are practicing the very underlying value of what it means to be a servant leader.

This point being made, there are great benefits that Community Schools bring to the school itself. Most of these benefits are directly related to the creation and sustenance of a positive school culture. Of particular significance is the fact that the benefits are reaped by the school long after the community involvement begins. Consider this; members of the community who otherwise would not be found in the schools go to the school for a particular community activity. While in the school, these community members see things that give them positive feelings. Maybe they see student work displayed that is of exceptionally high quality. Maybe they see artistic examples that show tremendous creativity and give a brief glimpse into the heart and soul of some of the students. Maybe they see signs advertising an upcoming pep rally, ball game, concert, or dance. All of these things illustrate for the community some of the positive things taking place in the school. For many of the community members, they bring back memories of positive school experiences they, themselves, enjoyed.

Now, an obvious benefit of this would be increased attention to the athletic and/or artistic components of the school program. That is, if more members of the community knew of athletic and artistic events, they would be more likely to attend. However, the more subtle benefit exists whether people attend these events or not. Simply knowing the positive things that go on in a school gives community members a more positive feeling about the school than they would have otherwise had. This, in turn, may lead to more positive things being said out in the community, which offers a great anecdote to negative publicity.

THE COALITION FOR COMMUNITY SCHOOLS

With the variety of Community Schools models in existence, the Coalition for Community Schools (www. communityschools.org) seeks to be an agency for bridging the ideas of the many organizations involved in creating Community Schools. Currently, there is a vast array of partners working with the coalition to advance the notion that there is tremendous value in schools operating as communities and for communities. Among the coalition's many partner organizations are the following:

- ♦ American Association of School Administrators
- ♦ American Federation of Teachers
- ♦ Collaborative for Integrated School Services
- ♦ Council of Chief State School Officers
- ♦ National Association of Elementary School Principals
- ♦ National Association of Secondary School Principals
- ♦ National Association of State Boards of Education
- ♦ National Coalition for Parent Involvement in Education
- ♦ National Community Education Association
- ♦ National Education Association
- ♦ National School Boards Association
- ♦ Corporation for National Service
  - Learn and Serve America
- ♦ U.S. Department of Education
  - National School-to-Work Office
  - Office of Education, Research and Improvement
  - Office of Elementary and Secondary Education
  - Office of the Secretary

- Office of Special Education Programs
- Safe and Drug-Free Schools Program
♦ U.S. Department of Health and Human Services
  - Administration for Children and Families
  - Centers for Disease Control and Prevention
  - Office of Adolescent Health
  - Office of Assistant Secretary for Planning and Evaluation
♦ U.S. Department of Housing and Urban Development
  - Office of University Partnerships
♦ U.S. Department of Justice
  - Office of Juvenile Justice and Delinquency Prevention

These organizations, as key stakeholders in American public education endorse, in large measure, the underlying concepts of Community Schools. They recognize two important elements. First, there is a great need for connectedness in our society. People need to feel connected to one another and to their community. When such connections exist, these agencies know, then people are more positive and productive. The experiences all readers have in schools surely confirm this. As mentioned in Chapter 4, the sense of community created in a classroom is a great determinant of how positive the culture will be. This, in turn, is a great determinant of how well students will achieve.

The second key understanding shared by many of these agencies is that our schools are centers of the community. In many ways, they are the hub of the giant wheel we call "community." This is not true solely because of location, but it also has a great deal to do with the school's role, as seen by members of society. Our schools are considered by many to be the "ticket" for citizens to achieve their dreams. Taking this ticket away from people just because they've reached a certain age is simply unacceptable. Instead, the ticket ought to represent a lifetime membership. Community Schools exist for all members of the community and are, consequently, redeemers of the citizens' lifetime memberships.

THE SCHOOL LEADER IN A COMMUNITY SCHOOL

Accepting the need for our schools to serve our communities should not in any significant way change the principal's role. In fact, as I have said, the extent to which a school serves its surrounding community is most often a decision that is out of the principal's hands. However, the beliefs and behaviors of the principal that correlate so well with positive school cultures are the very same beliefs and behaviors that help to create a sense of community within our schools.

As a principal, I always believed that members of our community as a whole should also be members of our school community. For this reason, whenever feasible, I encouraged all staff members to invite and involve the community in the education of our students. This led to many exciting learning experiences for our students, and it created a much greater level of understanding about our school's goals and purposes within the larger community. The important point to consider is that this did not create work for myself or any of my staff members. In fact, in many ways it reduced the amount of work required of all of us. Consider this example as an illustration:

The fourth grade teachers in a school I served as principal were getting ready to embark on a Health unit about the heart. Though this group of teachers was a highly skilled one and though we had a vast array of curricular materials in the school for them to use, the fourth grade teachers recognized that there were more knowledgeable people in the community about this topic. These same teachers understood that within our school were some staff members who had different understandings about the heart and its functions. They recognized that some of these colleagues could offer a great deal to the students in terms of enhancing their understanding. Below are some of the things these teachers did to enhance this experience for students.

- They involved the physical education teacher in their planning and subsequent teaching of the unit. This showed recognition that the physical education teacher had more expertise in the benefits of exercising the heart muscle than did the fourth grade teachers.

- They sought out assistance from the cafeteria staff. This showed a realization that the cafeteria staff members understood more about the benefits of proper nutrition than did the fourth grade teaching team.

- They contacted a cardiologist from the local hospital and asked that he come to school to speak with students about heart disease. He even brought a heart defibrillator and other medical equipment for students to examine. This was an excellent way to utilize the expertise found in the larger community.

- They brought in a parent who taught yoga classes and worked with individuals on stress reduction techniques. This parent, who also had expertise that the teachers did not possess, taught students an important lesson on the benefits of relaxation.

- They got calves' hearts from a local butcher. With the assistance of the science lab coordinator, students had an opportunity to closely examine these hearts as a close model to the human heart. In this way, community resources were further utilized.

While it may appear to some that a great deal of extra work was required to teach this unit, that simply is not the case. As these teachers discovered in making their initial contacts, members of the community were eager to assist. Several of them even commented that they had never been asked to be involved in the school's program before. Moreover, after they assisted, all involved community members stated that they would love to assist again in the future. By making a few simple telephone calls, these teachers made valuable connections between the school and the community. This, in turn, made it highly likely that our school would get support from these community members in the future.

In short, the opportunities for school personnel to involve the community in the educational goals of the school are endless. It begins with a commitment from the leader, though. Our schools, if they really want to enjoy positive relationships with our communities, must have leaders who understand the many benefits of community involvements. Utilizing the leadership behaviors outlined in Chapter 3, these school leaders must model the many ways in which community members can be involved in the school and the ways in which the school can assist the community. They must infuse these values into the culture of the school. As we know, when such values are exemplified in the mission and vision of the school, then they are much more likely to be exhibited by members of the school community.

In the giant patchwork quilt that we began creating at the beginning of this book, we must reserve spaces for squares that represent the community. We must understand that the quilt is strongest and most comforting when it is made up of more than just principals, teachers, non-teaching staff members, parents, and students. A quilt like that, represents a school that exists in isolation from the community in which it is located. When community members are included, the quilt's appeal becomes much broader, and it begins to be enjoyed by many more people.

Remember too, that the thread which binds these squares together is a positive school culture. The stronger the culture, the longer the quilt will last. The community must be an important part of any school's existence. It must be tightly bound to the school's goals, vision, and mission. When it is, we will have created positive school cultures for all. Not only will our schools be places where students can achieve, but everybody will know how students achieve and will work harmoniously toward that purpose.

SUMMARY OF KEY POINTS

- The sense of community that our schools must have implicitly implies that all stakeholders must work together in order that they may achieve together.

- Obstacles to creating a real sense of community exist for many of our schools.

- Organizations and members of our community need to recognize what they offer to our schools and what our schools offer to them before they will become involved.

- School leaders ought to think seriously about ways in which they can communicate the goals and accomplishments of their schools to community members outside of the normal school community.

- Schools are not merely institutions that teach children, but can and ought to be learning centers for the entire community because learning is a lifelong process.

- The beliefs and behaviors of the principal that correlate so well with positive school cultures are the very same beliefs and behaviors that help to create a sense of community within our schools.

8

BUILDING CONFIDENCE, INSPIRING TRUST: THE FUTURE OF PUBLIC EDUCATION IN AMERICA

The future of American public education is not bleak, as the nay sayers would have us believe. We certainly face challenges, but they are not insurmountable and we should not shy away from them in fear. Our focus must be on always doing that which is in the best interest of our students. I am telling you nothing new when I say that it is easy to become distracted by all the rhetoric regarding the educational problems, real or imagined, that we regularly face as a nation. Everybody reading this, without regard to your specific role in a school or the depth and breadth of your experiences, can relate to a feeling of pressure from constituents and the larger publics you deal with on a daily basis. Ours must be a business of optimism, however. Being in the business of education and doing our work on behalf of children requires us to always remain optimistic about public education's future. Frankly, I know of no other way.

In being optimistic, each one of us must not be blind to the fact that some things in our schools must get better. It is up to all of us, the educators, to see to it that this happens. The people in society who complain about what they perceive our failures to be, usually do so with what they perceive to be best for children in their minds. They usually want the same things that we all want; namely a quality education for the children who, in actuality, represent all of our futures. In this regard, we must understand that we are, in essence, educating the future leaders of America. This statement alone is what makes education the most important profession that I know of. In doing so, we are preparing children to enter an America that, in many ways, is yet to be discovered. We are attempting to train students for work that we, ourselves, do not yet understand. We are shaping the future, though we really do not know what the end product will be like. The task before us, as stated in the book's opening, is challenging. This fact should not inspire fear, but should instead lead to great excitement.

The study of school culture and the lessons we can learn from it will enable us to make decisions that are unquestionably in the best interests of the students we serve. For it is through school culture that we impart a sense of our mission and our commitments. It is through school culture that we proclaim what we believe in and what goals we have for our students. If we want students to be committed to success, then such a commitment must naturally permeate our culture. When it fails to do so, then it is not enough for us to command, as we too often do, that students succeed. We cannot make something so through edict, at least not something as large and profound as student success. We can only make bigger things happen by having their attainment at the heart of all our decisions, of all that we say, and of all that we do. Actions, indeed, speak louder than words. It is through our school culture that we give our actions a voice. We need school cultures that are committed to students' success and to utilizing all of our resources to make their success a reality.

Our study of school culture also shows us that we are most successful when we deal with individual needs in a collective manner. While this sounds like an oxymoron, its meaning is really quite clear. We must understand, to the best of our abilities, what it is that defines success and a sense of worth in the students we serve. For as we all know, success is defined differently by different people. While some define success in terms of a high grade point average or excellent attendance, there are others who measure success by incremental improvements or internal feelings of worth. The same quest for understanding must lead us to an examination of the motivating factors affecting the behavior of all staff members. We must discover ways to make schooling a successful experience for our staff, as well. Similarly, we must understand our parents. What do they and the rest of our community see as a vision for their youth? By dealing with all of these constituent groups and recognizing their contributions to school culture, we really can deal with individual needs in a collective manner. We must demonstrate that we really do have our fingers on the pulse of the parents and the community.

This knowledge, which we can never fully possess, allows us and propels us to create a collective set of beliefs and a collective vision for our school. Such beliefs and vision become the foundation for a culture's growth. Over time, as we collectively deal with individual needs, we create a school culture that is a positive one for our community. This culture, as we now recognize, must be sustained over time so that the behaviors associated with it become automatic and habitual.

It sounds so nebulous, but the concept is really quite simple. The creation, fostering, and sustenance of a positive school culture is everybody's responsibility. Any group can have a positive culture. It can only happen if the school leader believes and subsequently behaves in a manner which permits it, though. Equally important, a positive school culture can only exist when all stakeholder groups are part of it and are represented by it. In this regard, everybody is part of the leadership team, while paradoxically also being followers. They follow the collective mission of the school, but they also lead in the creation and in the advancement of the mission. This concept represents interdependency at its finest.

BUILDING CONFIDENCE

Many of the educators whom I have had the pleasure of working with, either as student, colleague, supervisor, or instructor have held the belief that the public does not trust the work that they do on behalf of children. These people have further believed that most Americans would give our public schools failing grades if they had the power to do so. These assumptions are often incorrect.

According to The 30th Annual Phi Delta Kappa/Gallup Poll of the Public's Attitudes Toward the Public Schools, 46 percent of the respondents give the schools in their own community a grade of A or B. In addition, 49 percent of those polled indicated a belief that the education children get today is better than the education they received, themselves. Contrast this with the lesser 43 percent who felt that they had received a better education than children are receiving today. It is apparent from this research that there is some strong public support for our schools.

This poll, with the purpose of providing those making decisions about schools with the data to be used as input in those decisions, shows us other interesting, thought-provoking trends, as well. Since the question was first asked in 1990, for example, the percentage of Americans who believe that public school parents should have more say in such aspects of school operation as selection and hiring of teachers and administrators, setting of their salaries, and selection of books for school libraries has increased significantly. This, at a time when 73 percent of those polled believe themselves to be either well informed or fairly well informed regarding local public schools.

This data, obviously open to different interpretations, tells me that while Americans by and large do feel that we are doing a good job and keeping them informed, they want an even greater voice in our governance. It is a natural byproduct of the information age in which we find ourselves. This is analogous to an experience that happens in my house from time to time. When my children go outside to play my wife and I always remind our two oldest, ages eight and six, to watch their younger sister who is two and a half. Even though we say this every time they go outside to play and even though they have always acted responsibly and done what we have asked of them, my wife and I still find ourselves looking out the window and listening closely as the children play. We believe that the two oldest children are doing a good job. Furthermore, we recognize that they keep us well informed if things go wrong outside. Nevertheless, love them as we do, we just do not quite trust their supervisory skills enough to remove ourselves completely from watching and listening.

I think the general public feels this way about our schools to some degree. And really, why shouldn't they? They are bombarded with reports that show us performing at levels below those of our counterparts in other industrialized nations. They see news reports that showcase violence and acts of hatred taking place in our schools. They see a generation that does not seem to value all that they valued when they were in school. These things are clearly not all our fault. In fact, many of them are gross misrepresentations of what is really going on in our schools. Nevertheless, the information, distorted as it may be, is out there. Furthermore, it represents the only information many members of the public get about us. We can hide our heads in the sand and curse the media for misrepresenting us, or we can be proactive. We can accept that the information is out there, and we can set the record straight accordingly. The challenge for us is to build the public's confidence in our work once again. We can do this, but only if we first invite them to our schools, make them a part of our culture, and tell them the truth.

SOMETIMES THE TRUTH HURTS

Telling the public the truth means many different things to many different people. What it does not mean is that we should complain to the public and assert that they do not understand and, thus misrepresent what we are doing in our schools. It also does not mean that we ought to attempt to tell the public that which we believe they want to hear. Instead, telling the truth means sharing our hardships, asking for assistance, and celebrating our successes. How many of you think that the public is aware of your successes? How many of you have programs at your schools, which promote the success of your students, but of which the general public in your community is unaware? How many of you have standardized test scores that reflect excellent achievement for your students given their ability, but do not measure up with scores in other schools in your region that obviously have different student populations?

The answers most of us give to the above questions indicate our need to more honestly inform the public of what we are doing well. In a recent poll of school superintendents, 75 percent indicated that they wished they had received more training in School-Community Relations. These individuals apparently feel that communicating with the general public, often through the media, is one of the greatest administrative concerns facing our schools. Many administrators claim that they simply do not have time to call the newspapers every time something good happens in their schools. These administrators are often the same people who lament that the newspapers do not cover the good news stories when they do take the time to call them, anyway. This fact is a widely used excuse among administrators who struggle with public relations issues. I maintain that leaders cannot afford *not* to continuously contact the newspapers in their area every time something good is happening in their schools. The fact that the media does not always respond when called is too weak an excuse to use for not doing something as important as this. Students, for example, do not always respond to the techniques we use in our schools, either instructional or in regards to behavior management. That does not, however, give us cause to cease trying, does it? If one of our goals is to involve the community in our schools, then we must make diligent attempts to include and welcome the media in our schools.

School leaders need a regular, purposeful plan for communicating with constituents. Such a plan must include regular media contacts, frequent written communication to parents, open houses and academic fairs, business partnerships, and requirements that staff members regularly contact parents with good news about students. These all are important elements of a plan that will lead to increased public understanding and confidence in what we are doing in our schools. Objectives of these elements are:

- ♦ To give the community vital information about what goes on in the schools.
- ♦ To give the school similar information about the community.
- ♦ To inform the community regarding new trends in education, perhaps nationwide.
- ♦ To secure community support for the school and its functions.
- ♦ To receive evaluative information from the community, relative to the school's goals.

- To establish and maintain the public's confidence in our schools.
- To foster and develop cooperation between the school and the community.
- To make the school an integral part of the community and the community an integral part of the school.

Open, honest, positive communication from the school to the community accomplishes these goals and invariably leads to increased public confidence. Securing information from the community, through parent telephone calls, business partnerships, and open houses provides the school staff with vital information about the degree of confidence that the community has. It is a tremendous responsibility, but it is of paramount importance in building up the public's confidence in our education systems.

Not all of this responsibility needs to fall squarely on the shoulders of the principal. When such ideas are consistent with the school's mission, they become the responsibility of everybody. I know of several schools that have volunteer parents to assist in some of these tasks, for example. Parents can work with businesses to secure donations, or they can take on leadership roles in producing school newsletters to name only a few appropriate responsibilities. Many of the tasks, as the above explanations illustrate, are the responsibility of staff members. Remember, while all stakeholders must be included in the development of the school's mission statement, they must also involve themselves in carrying out the school's mission.

At the risk of making this chapter too much like a public relations textbook, this point must be made clear. We cannot improve public confidence in our schools by remaining quiet. Nor can we improve confidence by longing for the "good old days", real or imagined, when people allegedly had greater confidence in us than they appear to have today. We must, instead, engage in meaningful two-way communication with our public. This includes informing them of the many great things we are doing, asking for assistance with our struggles, and listening to their concerns.

INSPIRING TRUST

More than just building confidence, educational leaders are charged with inspiring the trust of all stakeholders in order to be successful. A leader who is not trusted will find his/her ability to lead and inspire others to be drastically diminished. The shared commitments and confluence of values that are so important to a positive school culture will not be present in schools in which there is little trust. Before somebody is willing to align their beliefs with yours and work with you toward common goals, they must trust you. They must believe that you mean what you say. They must have no questions regarding your openness, your honesty, or your trustworthiness.

In many ways, it is easier for an educational leader to earn the trust of staff members, students, and parents, than it is to earn the trust of strangers, or community members who never venture into the school. These people, who we find difficult to reach do read newspapers and watch television, though. They also drive by your school and make observations regularly. They receive some information that forms the basis for their feelings and the level of understanding they have about your school. If you, as an educational leader, are to impact these feelings and understandings, then you must inspire the trust of community members.

The most obvious way in which educational leaders do this is through honesty. As discussed earlier, even when the truth is painful to tell, it is better than the alternative. In many ways, one lie outdoes the accomplishments of a whole lifetime of truths. School leaders are not only urged never to lie, but they also must never give the perception that they are lying. Since perception in many cases is reality, then any time the public perceives a school staff member to be lying the damage is already done.

Covering up and making excuses are two examples of behaviors that the public will often interpret, or perceive, as lying. This is an important point to pay attention to. Reactive people tend to cover things up and make excuses with much more frequency than do proactive people. Proactive people seek opportunities to discuss an issue long before it becomes a problem. Consider the following example as an illustration:

You are a principal in one of the lowest achieving schools in your region, as measured by the statewide standardized testing. The results of tests for all schools in the region have been reported to the local newspaper, and you know that reporters will soon be calling to get your reaction. What do you do? A proactive person and a reactive person will deal with this situation quite differently. Below are sample reactions:

♦ Proactive

As soon as your test results arrive, you begin analyzing the data, looking for trends and signs that relate to your school's academic program. You involve key constituents in this analysis and expediently share the results with the staff. You begin preparing your reaction in layman's terms, as you recognize that you will need to share and interpret these test results with many different people. Knowing that the local newspaper has received or will shortly be receiving the test results, you call and ask to speak to the education reporter. You explain the results as honestly as possible, in language that is clear. You make no excuses, but you inform the reporter of both the benefits and the limitations of standardized testing. You explain the reasons why you and your staff believe the scores are not great, and you quickly share your plan for improvement. If such a plan is not yet developed, you openly acknowledge that it is in the development phase and you urge the reporter to come and visit your school frequently as you plan and implement it. You involve parents in these discussions from the onset, and you give the reporter the names of some parents that the reporter can speak to regarding your school and its performance.

♦ Reactive

Upon receipt of the test results, you feel a sense of doom in the pit of your stomach. The scores are never good, you reason. Why should it be any different this time around? You give the results to teachers, and you ask them to please explain to you why they are so poor. Just then, you realize that reporters will be calling soon. You instruct the secretarial staff to put no calls from reporters through. Instead, they are to tell reporters that you are in a meeting, and instruct them to call you back at a different time. In your mind, you begin reviewing the excuses. Attendance in your school is poor. Kids of today just don't care. Parents need to be more involved. The test is an invalid measure of your school's curriculum. The list goes on and on. Speaking to this reporter is something you dread. Receiving telephone calls from parents after the scores are released is even worse. This is one of those days in which you wonder why you ever went into education in the first place.

The scenario I have given as an example is not at all far-fetched. In fact, I am confident that many readers can relate to the issue I have presented through some firsthand experience. The two reactions, from my observations, are not far-fetched either. Maybe you know a leader whose description fits each of the responses. It ought to be clear, however, that the proactive response is going to be much better at inspiring trust in your school. While some of the elements in the reactive response may be true, lengthy discussions of them will lead nowhere. There is no point in repeatedly identifying the problem when we are faced with a dilemma, as the reactive example does. We need to be about solutions. We know what the problems are. Proactive people work on solutions immediately. I know that I have far greater trust in leaders who try to solve problems than I do in those who merely whine about them.

We further inspire community members to trust us when we take our message to them. Speaking before local civic organizations about your accomplishments as well as your struggles is an excellent technique for building trust. In the example of the poor test scores, think of the gains achieved by going to the community at the beginning and explaining the results. Further gains are achieved in explaining innovative ideas the school staff has for improving things. Still greater gains are realized when you enlist the help of these civic organizations in accomplishing your goals.

THE FUTURE
OF EDUCATION

Can education continue to exist, as we currently know it? This question is asked time and time again by those who concern themselves regularly with the future of education. Perhaps a better question to ask is, "Should education continue to exist, as we currently know it?"

Whether we believe that society drives education or that education drives society, one thing is clear. As society changes, so does education. When education becomes "stuck" or mired in techniques and beliefs that are reflective of the past is when it comes under the sharpest criticism. If you disagree, consider this simple question: What would the public's perception likely be of a school that is not sufficiently wired to the Internet?

Ironically, at the same time, we hear pundits lament that our schools need to go "back to the basics" if we are to achieve at a level, real or imagined, that we once achieved. Just as there are people who deplore society's changes, there will always be those who lament education's.

This leads to a great deal of confusion regarding education's future. Will we continue to emphasize the basics, as some claim we should? Or is education's future one of change? How will technology shape our educational institutions? Will increased focus on accountability achieve the opposite result from that which it intends—namely, less focus on the real meaning of education?

I could give you my prediction, just as you could share your own. However, this book is not about predictions, it is about certainties. Whatever the future of education is in this country, it will be better if we remain focused on the benefits of positive school cultures. If we remain cognizant that students achieve more in schools that have positive cultures, then the advent of new technologies or the focus on new measures of accountability will fit in with, not detract from, our mission. We will embrace change with a focus on remaining positive.

Likewise, if we remain constant in our belief that the entire community ought to be involved in education, then we will work together through whatever changes the future tides bring in. Just as our forefathers needed a sense of community to feel important, our children will continue to feel this need well into the future. By not forgetting this, we begin to prepare ourselves for whatever the future brings. Students will always benefit from schools with positive cultures. Furthermore, the creation of such schools will always be well within our control.

CONCLUSIONS

Summing up the general knowledge base regarding school culture is difficult, to say the least. There are, however, a few key concepts underlying the pages in this book that are worth delineating. Post these concepts where you will regularly see them, or better yet, commit them to memory. They are ideas that we simply cannot afford to forget. They are:

- ◆ School culture affects the behavior and achievement of all students.
- ◆ School culture does not happen automatically and instantly; it is created and sustained over time.
- ◆ All people in the school community can manipulate school culture. As such, they all have responsibility for its maintenance.
- ◆ The principal is the key, for the principal's behaviors are the most influential.

- Teachers are the most important adults in the process, for they have the greatest, deepest contact with children during the school day.

- Parents, as their child's first teacher, play integral roles in their child's perception of school's value. Involving them and enlisting their help are vital elements to the creation and sustenance of a positive school culture.

- Students cannot be forgotten in our journeys to create positive cultures. Our schools, we cannot forget, exist for the students.

- The community needs the school and the school needs the community. When the community and the school work in tandem, then school culture is strengthened.

- School cultures are unique. No two schools are, or should be, exactly alike.

- Because of its ability to provide focus and clarity, culture is the tie that binds the school together.

- Lasting change requires an understanding of the culture.

- Though it must constantly be examined, and potentially altered, cultural change is a slow process.

The concept of school culture and its application in our schools is, in many ways, complex in its simplicity. The richness and durability of school cultures are fascinating and give our schools their life. The ramifications of school culture are great in regards to student achievement and the realization of educational goals and purposes. It has become further apparent that school culture is the very soul of our schools.

Throughout this book, I have attempted to bring the research regarding school culture alive for you. I have tried to sum it up and apply it to schooling through the eyes that I have been given. As all learning is an interactive process, you have been charged with the responsibility of seeing through my eyes, in many instances. Furthermore, you have been required to take my words and the images they have created and see them come alive with your own eyes. That continues to be the real challenge.

I hope you will use your eyes and transfer the visions our students need to those you work with in the schools. I hope that school culture now has a deeper, more profound meaning for you. More importantly, I hope you cherish the uniqueness of your school's culture. Understand its relationship with student achievement, modify it accordingly, but cherish it. You are a part of it, and it is an important part of you.

Creating a positive school culture is your responsibility. Continue building relationships that help students achieve and we will all see lasting school improvement. The task before us is not so monumental. It is so very important, though. Our children, and thus our future, depend on our ability. I, for one, remain eternally optimistic.

SUMMARY OF KEY POINTS

♦ The creation, fostering, and sustenance of a positive school culture is everybody's responsibility.

♦ A positive school culture can only exist when all stakeholder groups are part of it and are represented by it.

♦ The challenge for us is to build the public's confidence in our work once again.

♦ School leaders need a regular, purposeful plan for communicating with constituents.

♦ More than just building confidence, educational leaders are charged with inspiring the trust of all stakeholders in order to be successful.

♦ Creating a positive school culture is your responsibility.

REFERENCES

Bandura, A. (1986). *Social foundations of thought and action: A social cognitive theory.* Englewood Cliffs, NJ: Prentice-Hall.

Bissell, B. (1992). *The paradoxical leader.* Paper presented at the Missouri Leadership Academy, Columbia, MO.

Blankenhorn, D. (1995). Pay, papa, pay. *National Review, 47*(6), 34–42.

Bohm, D. (1996). *On dialogue.* London: Routledge.

Bower, M. (1997). *The will to lead: Running a business with a network of leaders.* Boston: Harvard Business School Press.

Boyer, E.L. (1983). *High school: A report of the Carnegie Foundation for the Advancement of Teaching.* New York: Harper & Row.

Braddock, J.H., Dawkins, M.P., & Wilson, G. (1995). Intercultural contact and race relations among American youth. In W.D. Hawley & A. Jackson (Eds.), *Toward a common destiny: Improving race relations in America.* San Francisco: Jossey-Bass.

Buell, N. (1992). Building a shared vision—the principal's leadership challenge. *NASSP Bulletin, 76*(542), 88–92.

Butler, D. (1995). *Improving school learning environments: A resource manual of knowledge strategies.* Memphis, TN: Memphis University Center for Research in Educational Policy (ERIC Document Reproduction Service No. ED 386 787).

Chalkey, G. (1989). Smart moves better body, better brain? *American Health, 8*(10), 32.

Cicourel, A.V. (1974). *Language use and school performance.* New York: Academic Press.

Covey, S.R. (1989). *The seven habits of highly effective people.* New York: Simon & Schuster.

Covey, S.R. (1990). *Principle centered leadership.* New York: Simon & Schuster.

Covey, S.R. (1997). *The seven habits of highly effective families.* New York: Golden Books.

Deal, T.E., & Kennedy, A.A. (1982). *Corporate cultures.* Reading, MA: Addison-Wesley.

DeLeon, J. & Medina, B. (1997). A model project for identifying rural gifted and talented students in the visual arts. *Rural Special Education Quarterly,16*(4), 16–23.

Findley, B. & Findley, D. (1992). Effective schools: The role of the principal. *Contemporary Education, 63*(2), 102–104.

Fiore, D.J. (2000). Behaviors of a principal directly influence a school's culture. *The Journal of Educational Relations, 21*(1), 5–16.

Fiore, D.J. (1999). *The relationship between principal effectiveness and school culture in elementary schools.* (Doctoral dissertation, Indiana State University, 1999).

Foriska, T.J. (1994). The principal as instructional leader: Teaming with teachers for student success. *Schools in the Middle, 3*(3), 31–34.

Frase, L.E., & Melton, R.G. (1992). Manager or participatory leader? What does it take? *NASSP Bulletin, 76*(540), 17–24.

Fullan, M.G. (1994). Coordinating top-down and bottom-up strategies for educational reform. In R.F. Elmore & S.H. Furhman (Eds.): *The governance of curriculum: The 1994 Yearbook of the Association for Supervision and Curriculum Development.* Alexandria, VA: Association for Supervision and Curriculum Development

Fyans, L. & Maehr, M. (1990). *School culture, student ethnicity, and motivation.* Urbana, IL: The National Center for School Leadership (ED 327-947).

Ginott, H.G. (1972). *Teacher and child: A book for parents and teachers.* New York: Macmillan.

Greenfield, W.D. (1985). *Instructional leadership: Muddles, puzzles, and promises.* The Doyne M. Smith Lecture, University of Georgia, 1985.

Greenleaf, R. (1977). *Servant leadership: A journey into the nature of legitimate power and greatness.* New York: Paulist Press.

Heckman, P.E. (1988). Understanding school culture. The ecology of school renewal. *Eighty-Fifth Yearbook.* Chicago: National Society for the Study of Education.

Heckman, P.E. (1993). School restructuring in practice: Reckoning with the culture of school. *International Journal of Educational Reform, 2*(3), 263–271.

Herzberg, G. (1993). *The motivation to work.* New Brunswick, NJ: Transaction.

Hopkins, D., Ainscow, M., & West, M. (1994). *School improvement in an era of change.* London: Cassell.

Kaplan, L., & Evans, M.W. (1997). Changing school environment: Restructuring one Virginia high school. *NASSP Bulletin, 81*(589), 1–9.

Kelly, P., Brown, S., Butler, A., Gittens, P., Taylor, C., & Zeller, P. (1998). A place to hang our hats. *Educational Leadership, 56*(1), 62–64.

Kilmann, R.H. (1989). *Managing beyond the quick fix.* San Francisco: Jossey-Bass.

Kohl, H. (1998). *The discipline of hope: Learning from a lifetime of teaching.* New York: Simon and Schuster.

Levine, D., & Lezotte, L. (1990). *Unusually effective schools: A review and analysis of research and practice.* Madison, WI: The National Center for Research and Development.

McEwan, E.K. (1998). *How to deal with parents who are angry, troubled, afraid, or just plain crazy.* Thousand Oaks, CA: Corwin Press.

Merriam-Webster's new collegiate dictionary. (2000). Online source: www.m-w.com/cgibin/dictionary.

Morgan, G. (1986). *Images of organization.* Newbury Park, CA: Sage Publications.

Prociando, M.E., & Fisher, C.B. (1992). Contemporary families: A handbook for school professionals. New York: Teachers College Press.

Riley, R.W. (1994). Ingredient for success: Parent involvement. *Teaching Pre K-8, 25*(1), 12.

Sarason, S.B. (1982). *The culture of the school and the problem of change.* Boston: Allyn & Bacon.

Schlechty, P. (1997). *Inventing better schools: An action plan for educational reform.* San Francisco: Jossey-Bass.

Sergiovanni, T.J. (1995). The principalship: A reflective practice perspective. Needham Heights, MA: Simon and Schuster.

Sergiovanni, T.J. (1996). *Leadership for the schoolhouse.* San Francisco: Jossey-Bass.

Smylie, M.A. (1991). Organizational cultures of schools: Concept, content, and change. In S. Conley & B. Cooper (Eds.): *The School as a work environment: Implications for reform.* Boston: Allyn & Bacon.

Stolp, S. (1996). Leadership for school culture. *Emergency Librarian, 23*(3), 30–31.

Sutherland, F. (1994). *Teachers' perceptions of school climate.* Chicago, IL: Chicago State University (ERIC Document Reproduction Service No. ED 379 214).

Sweeney, J. (1986). Developing a strong culture: The key to school improvement. *National Forum of Educational Administration and Supervision Journal 3,* 134–143.

The National Data Book. Statistical abstract of the United States: 118th edition. (1998). Baton Rouge, LA: Claitors.

The 30th annual Phi Delta Kappa/Gallup Poll of the public's attitudes toward the public schools. (1998). Online source: www.pdkintl.org/kappan/kp9809-a.htm

Trice, H.M. (1985). *Rites and ceremonials in organizational cultures: Research into the sociology of organizations.* Greenwich, CT: JAI Press.

U.S. Bureau of Labor Statistics (1999). Online source: http://stats.bls.gov

Whitaker, M.E. (1997). Principal leadership behaviors in school operations and change implementations in elementary schools in relation to climate (Doctoral dissertation, Indiana State University, 1997).

Whitaker, T.C. (1999). *Dealing with difficult teachers.* Larchmont, NY: Eye on Education.